D1483093

UNITED STATES PT-BOATS OF WORLD WAR II IN ACTION

UNITED STATES PT-BOATS OF WORLD WAR II IN ACTION

by

FRANK D. JOHNSON

Line illustrations by John Batchelor

BLANDFORD PRESS

Poole, Dorset

First published in the UK 1980 by Blandford Press,
Link House, West Street, Poole, Dorset, BH15 1LL

Copyright © 1980 Blandford Books Ltd

Reprinted 1983

Distributed in the United States by
Sterling Publishing Co., Inc.,
2 Park Avenue, New York, N.Y. 10016

All rights reserved. No part of this book may be reproduced
or transmitted in any form or by any means, electronic
or mechanical, including photocopying, recording or any
information storage and retrieval system, without permission
in writing from the Publisher.

ISBN 0 7137 1025 X (Hardback)
ISBN 0 7137 1405 0 (Paperback)

British Library Cataloguing in Publication Data

Johnson, Frank
    United States P.T. Boats of World War 2 in action.
    — (In action series).
    1. World War, 1939–45 — Naval operations, American
    2. Torpedo-boats — United States — History
    I. Title II. Series
    940.54'59'73   D773

Designed by Vigo.
Filmset in 'Monotype' Plantin and printed in Great Britain
by BAS Printers Limited, Over Wallop, Hampshire.

Printed in U.S.A. by Arcata Graphics
Kingsport, TN.

Contents

Preface

This book is a history of the development, production and major combat deployments of United States Navy motor torpedo boats during World War Two. An integral part of the work is over two hundred photographs, many of which have never before been published. This book is by no means a complete operational history, but rather attempts to detail the highlights of the most notable combat operations. For a more complete record of the day-to-day operations, combat and otherwise, of all PT-Boat squadrons throughout World War Two, readers may wish to obtain a copy of the official United States Navy history of PT-Boats in World War Two, *At Close Quarters*. Written by Captain Robert J. Bulkeley, the work was first published by the government in 1962. With few exceptions it is accurate, and details operations in some of the less interesting deployments (from the standpoint of there being little or no combat involved) such as the Aleutians, Midway, the English Channel and the south coast of France. American boats did engage the Germans to a certain extent in the English Channel and were active, for instance, during the Normandy landings. But the real story of the English Channel torpedo boat war is largely the history of the British MTB squadrons, a story which is beyond the scope of this work.

One thing that the reader may wish to keep in mind is that the concept of a PT-Boat force as was originally planned before the war was indeed that of a weapons system. It presupposed adequate numbers of boats, properly maintained and armed with effective weapons. At the beginning of the war, when enemy capital ship targets were plentiful, the American boats that reached the combat areas had not one of these factors working in their favor. PT-Boats were indeed a viable defensive weapons concept in the pre-radar era of 1937. They were even more deadly in the later stages of the war when radar became standard equipment aboard PT-Boats – and they remained so as long as enemy ships were not similarly equipped.

It is interesting to note that at the end of the war both advocate and foe of the PT-Boat concept could effectively argue that the war had demonstrated the validity of their respective positions. That the boats became very useful in the later stages of the war as barge and lighter busters cannot be argued. But as ship sinkers their record was questionable. Or was it? They did manage to sink numerous destroyers and perhaps even a cruiser or two. But in examining any one deployment, one must ask the question, what was their goal? In virtually every campaign where PT-Boats met the enemy they did what they were asked to do. Luckily, events never developed to the point where PT-Boats were asked to intercept Japanese aircraft-carriers standing off Los Angeles or San Francisco.

I would like to acknowledge the help of the following individuals in the preparation of this work: Captain Hugh Robinson, USN Ret., Robert L. Searles, John M. Searles, Lester H. Gamble, Rollin E. Westholm, Henry S. Taylor, 'Boats' Newberry of the PT-Boat Museum, Victor Chun, John Reilly and Robert Cressman.

Frank D. Johnson

I
Origins

The years of the late nineteenth and early twentieth centuries were the age of invention. Advances in engineering, particularly in metallurgy and metal working, brought forth a mechanized age that would at the same time prove to be the blessing and the curse of modern man.

United States Patrol Torpedo Boat 23 was moored, on the morning of 7 December 1941, at the Pearl Harbor Submarine Base. The 77 foot long, mahogony-hulled boat, built by the Electric Boat Company of Bayonne, New Jersey, sat low and deadly looking in the water, her gracefully smooth curves suggestive of the high speeds she and her five sisters moored alongside could make.

Torpedoman First Class George Huffman and Gunner's Mate First Class Joy Van Zyll de Jong were lounging on the deck of PT-23, enjoying a magnificent Hawaiian Sunday morning. No great note was taken of a group of aircraft passing overhead; morning patrols over the vast military complex were a common enough occurrence. But all similarity between this flight and what could be considered a common occurrence abruptly ended when the two men observed that these particular aircraft were dropping bombs.

PT sailors volunteered for their assignments. The Navy considered service aboard its glamorous new 'mosquito boats' to be strenuous duty, and the choice of crewmen was based in no small part on aggressiveness and physical agility. Huffman and de Jong wasted no time in demonstrating these traits as both men scrambled for the two twin .50 caliber machine-gun turrets mounted amidships on the 23 boat. The two men charged their guns, and as a low-flying 'Kate' torpedo plane droned by, its three-man Japanese crew was rudely surprised by a hundred one-inch-long steel missiles raking their mount from one end to the other. PT-23's .50 caliber slugs slammed into the Kate's big radial engine which immediately coughed, belched smoke and then lost power. The two men aboard the PT-Boat had the immense satisfaction of watching their target nose over and crash in flames near Kuahua Island. Moments later hits were registered on yet

another torpedo plane which obliged by exploding into a ball of fire to fall behind the submarine base.

While it is difficult to say whether a PT-Boat drew first blood for the United States Navy in this moments-old war, it is safe to say that this action was indeed the baptism of fire for a small and dashing craft that would, in a few short months, be the darling of the American press and public. Interestingly enough, while these small craft were designed as torpedo boats, this first action involving only automatic weapons was an omen of the ultimate employment these boats would find.

As the aerial attack on Pearl Harbor continued that December morning, crewmembers of eleven other PT-Boats were not far behind PT-23 in swinging into action with their anti-aircraft batteries. These dozen boats comprised Motor Torpedo Boat Squadron 1, one of but three such squadrons making up the total motor torpedo boat strength of the United States Navy in late 1941.

Fate had much in store for Squadrons 2 and 3 as well. As the first Japanese bombs fell, MTB Squadron 2 was fitting out its eleven boats in the New York Navy Yard in preparation for shipment aboard aircraft ferry ships to the Panama Canal, an area considered ideal for the implementation of small torpedo-carrying craft. Although the war would never come to Panama, these same boats would begin a grueling test of combat ten months later in the Solomon Islands.

The last group of boats on hand as the United States went to war were stationed in the Philippines and belonged to Motor Torpedo Boat Squadron 3, skippered by a man who would soon become the foremost figure in United States PT-Boat warfare, Lt John D. Bulkeley. The six boats of the under-strength squadron based at the Cavite Navy

Yard on Manila Bay would soon come to symbolize American courage and perseverance to the people at home who so desperately wanted something to cheer about during those dark days of early 1942.

Such was the lineup for these curious little hybrids of the United States Navy as the world squared off for what would be the greatest armed conflict man had yet experienced. They would go on to play their own definite and important part in the conflict, not so much as critical elements in the assurance of ultimate victory, but rather as tools for bringing what was soon considered a foregone conclusion to a speedier end, with a reduction in war's greatest cost – lives.

The accomplishments of the PT-Boats in the service of the American Navy during World War Two will be duly chronicled here. But any history of these craft must begin with an explanation of what the boats were and how they came to be. Indeed, that is one of the purposes of this book.

★   ★   ★   ★

In 1866 the Englishman Robert Whitehead successfully demonstrated his underwater, self-propelled 'fish' torpedo to Austrian naval officials. At the time the talented Whitehead was acknowledged as one of Austria's foremost marine engineers. Although the original idea of a self-propelled torpedo had been advanced to him by an Austrian naval officer several years earlier, it was Whitehead's application of the principle and his continued experimentation that resulted in a truly remarkable mechanical achievement for the time.

Although some fourteen feet long and weighing nearly 400 lbs, the first successful Whitehead torpedo powered by a compressed-air motor could carry less than 20 lbs of explosive under 1,000 yards at a mere seven knots. The Austrian Navy pur-

A truly fine example of PT-Boat photography shows two Squadron 1 boats idling out of Pearl Harbor during April 1942. The picture is taken from directly beside the plexiglass blister of the starboard-side, .50 caliber machine-guns of one boat, and PT-25 is seen in the background. The plexiglass blisters were soon removed along with their hydraulic drive mechanisms for traversing the mounts.

chased Whitehead's design, but not on an exclusive basis, and this gave the designer a free hand in peddling his wares. It did not take men of overly great vision to see the implications of such a weapon, especially as its performance and destructive ability continued to grow with the introduction of improved models. In 1871 Whitehead demonstrated and managed to sell rights for the manufacture of his torpedo to the most powerful and decidedly conservative navy in the world. Great Britain's Royal Navy paid Whitehead the tidy sum of £15,000 for his invention, thus setting in motion a chain of events that would have a revolutionary effect on naval warfare. Within a decade virtually every navy of any consequence, and many formerly of no consequence, would be equipped with torpedoes and a suitable method for

their delivery – primarily in the form of small (under 100 ft) steam-powered launches and boats appropriately dubbed 'torpedo boats'.

As the torpedo was an 'independent' weapon and could be delivered from any platform big enough to support it, the weapons, with the associated launching tubes, were installed in all manner of craft. As the weapon's development achieved new heights of lethality prior to World War One, it was introduced into yet another wonder of technology, the submarine. The resulting marriage of weapon and platform would initiate a well chronicled path of destruction unlike anything seen before in naval warfare.

The concurrent proliferation of 'torpedo boats' in the last years of the 19th century spawned still another type of craft that would begin life as the 'torpedo boat destroyer' (the first two words were soon dropped) and whose value and versatility would allow it to survive to this day as the most numerous modern surface ship type afloat.

The development of reliable gasoline-powered internal combustion engines with relatively decent power-to-weight ratios was another turning-point with regard to man's ability to make war. Such engines could power vehicles to travel over the land at great speeds, they could power machines that were able to fly through the air, and they could power small boats – occasionally at speeds previously unheard of on the water.

Much of the credit for the development of small fast motorboats must go to the British, with the Americans, Italians and French following close behind. Yachting had become a very popular sport in Britain, France and the United States during the 1880s and 1890s and, as with any popular activity, numerous 'official' organizations were founded. Racing became a popular pastime among the yachtsmen, leading eventually to sanctioned sporting events. As steam-powered launches became widespread as small auxiliaries carried aboard the larger craft, it was found that they too were fun to race. As reasonably reliable petroleum-powered engines became available around the turn of the century, many of these steam launches were converted to gasoline power – and they were in turn entered in competition.

By 1903 such motorboat racing became so popular that Sir Alfred Harmsworth sponsored a racing event to which he donated a trophy bearing his name. Harmsworth's trophy soon became known as the British International Trophy, awarded each year to the winning national motorboat team, and based on a number of events run against teams from other countries. The prestigious award came to be administered by the Motor Yacht Club of England under rules worked up by the newly formed Marine Motor Association in the United Kingdom and concurrently agreed to by another new body on the other side of the Atlantic, the American Power Boat Association. It would be due in no small part to the efforts of the members of these two associations that Great Britain and the United States would have an invaluable bank of information on which to draw forty years later. Step by step the racers, each seeking that competitive edge, would innovate and improve their designs and equipment, and virtually every one of these innovations would be incorporated in wartime designs.

The first important breakthrough came as a result of ever increasing engine horsepower output per given weight. Early on, all motor-

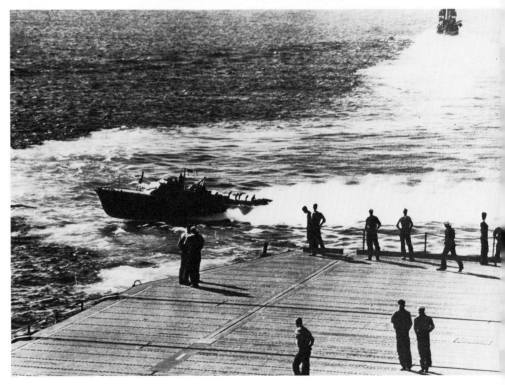

Top
PT-28 refuels at the Pearl Harbor gas dock during April 1942. The covered piece of equipment on the tripod is a Lewis .30 caliber machine-gun. Note that the porthole windows in the front of the charthouse have been covered over with a piece of canvas. Later, all windows were simply painted over to prevent light leakage. Three months after this photograph was taken PT-28 was sent to the Aleutians with seven of her sisters where they would operate as the only PTs in that theater until the arrival of Squadron 13's Higgins boats during March of the following year. With no forced air heating equipment, life bordered on the unbearable aboard the Elco boats in the Aleutians. PT-28 was eventually lost in an Aleutian storm during January 1943.

Bottom
Dicing with aircraft carriers was a lot of fun if nothing else. Here a Squadron 1 77 ft Elco cuts directly across the bow of a carrier off Pearl Harbor. Note the carrier's escorting destroyer up ahead.

powered race boats were of the displacement hull type. These boats cut through the water as they moved forward – displacing it, as it were. A typical displacement hull has a maximum practical hull speed. Any attempt to make such a hull travel faster through the water through the application of additional power generally results in very little added speed, most of the excess horsepower being dissipated in the effect of simply forcing the boat's stern further and further down into the trough of water created by its passing. Displacement hulls generally have rounded bottoms. The logical solution to keeping the stern from sinking as more power was added was to flatten and widen a boat's bottom as it neared the stern, thus creating a larger area of contact with the water and a greater resistance to sinking. The application of this principle was most notably demonstrated in the design offered by the American Clinton Crane for a 1907 challenge to the British International Trophy. His boat, *Dixie*, won the race at a 27 knot clip and for the first time brought the coveted British International Trophy to America. It was only the beginning of the fierce and very popular com-

petition between the two nations in this event.

The day of the fully planing speedboat was close at hand. The basic principles involved in making a boat skim over the water, as opposed to plowing through it, had been generally recognized for some years. But engines of sufficient power and low weight were required, as was a basic method of hull construction that would produce a light but strong package. Previously small-boat construction was accomplished in the same manner in which any wooden ship would be built, from the keel up. By 1905 several builders, most notably the Englishman Linton Hope, were experimenting with the idea of building motor boats based on the strength inherent in two heavy engine bearers which ran the length of the boat. As such, the boats were keelless. Heavy built up sides were replaced by a series of light-weight ribs, attached securely to the central engine bearers, over which a light-weight wooden skin was applied creating what was at least partially analogous to a monocoque fuselage.

Even the manner of attaching the outer skin took on innovative proportions when a

It had been decided in late 1941 to reinforce the six boats of Squadron 3 in the Philippines with six more boats, elements of Squadron 1. This reinforcement group was transiting the Pacific and happened to be in Pearl Harbor on the morning of 7 December 1941. Consequently, that is where they stayed for some time to come. This view shows several of the squadron's boats (including, from left to right, PTs 20, 21 and 23) tied up at Pearl City during April 1942. The boats ran patrols off the islands during the uncertain early months of the war.

method developed by the English designer S.E. Saunders began to catch on with racers. Saunders developed the principle of building the outer hull from progressive diagonal laminations of thin strips of mahogany and cedar, each successive layer secured to the one below. This accomplished two purposes. First, it made possible a weight saving of the order of 35 per cent using between five to eight layers of covering. Second, it allowed the engineer a new degree of flexibility in designing more radically shaped curved forms, the resultant experimentation in hull shape then leading to ever improving performance.

By 1910 the racers had reasonably powerful and reliable engines and the construction sophistication to build light, strong hulls. These factors were vital to the PT-Boats to come. But now, rather than refining the planing of mono-hull shapes, all racing hull design attention seemed to shift into a stepped hull configuration or what, more accurately, amounted to hydroplanes.

The British International Trophy specified that competition boats should be under 40 ft in length. Now the stepped hull hydroplane is a marvellous way of making the

most of the available horsepower. But a hydroplane is a very poor performing design at lower speeds where the planing sponsons have no effect. What is more, the hydroplaning effect is best utilized in smaller craft operating on sheltered waters. Rough water is not the forte of the hydroplane. Finally, while straight-line performance may be spectacular, hydroplanes have never been noted for their turning and maneuvering stability.

Even with its inherent shortcomings, the stepped hull motor-racing boat was engineered to a high degree of performance epitomized by such boats as *Miranda IV* of 1910 and *Maple Leaf IV* of 1912. Both craft were designed by the Thornycroft Company, a name that would become famous in the annals cf motor torpedo boat builders in the years to come. *Maple Leaf IV* would win the British International Trophy in 1912 and 1913 and would be the first racing boat to hit 50 knots, powered by her two 400 hp twelve-cylinder engines. While the hull utilized a single step amidships, the step was small and the smooth hull form was virtually integral from bow to stern. What is more, the bow section of the boat displayed a decidedly concave cross-section. This boat was an important step in the development of the seagoing, planing mono-hulled speedboat.

Sabres were beginning to rattle in Europe, and as World War One approached notable accomplishments in motor boat design had taken place in other countries as well. Perhaps most important, the famous Lürssen

yard in Germany built an experimental 31 foot speedboat dubbed *Boncourt*. With a top speed of 43 knots, the Germans fitted her to fire torpedoes. Although not the first motor boat to be so fitted, she was most certainly the fastest. In fact, Yarrow and Thornycroft of England and the Standard Boat Company of America had all produced, as early as 1905, small torpedo-carrying motor boats of between 40 to 90 feet, a number of which were results of orders from Russia and a few as one-off private ventures. But with top speeds of the order of 10 knots, they were of little strategic importance at the time of their delivery.

WORLD WAR ONE

World War One saw a proliferation of small fast torpedo-carrying motor boats. The British, Italian and German navies all became significantly involved in the operation of these craft, and some notable successes were achieved.

The British formula resulted in the Coastal Motor Boat or CMB. Designed and built in a number of different versions (to a maximum length of 55 ft) by Thornycroft, the CMB's basic lines were a direct adaptation and scaling up of the *Miranda IV* single-step hydroplane racer. Depending upon engine installation, the craft were capable of from 33 to 40 knots in calm seas. Unfortunately, the English Channel was seldom calm enough for high-speed running. Typically, the torpedo

PT-42 is gassed up at the Pearl Harbor fueling dock during April 1942. As one of the boats of Squadron 1 sent to the Hawaiian Islands just before the war, this boat was still resting in her cradle aboard the docked transport *Ramapo* on 7 December 1941.

Two Squadron 1 boats patrol off Pearl Harbor with the USS *Hornet* in the background. This is probably one of the most widely circulated PT-Boat photographs in existence.

was carried in a trough in the stern and was slid off the stern backwards while the boat headed for the target at high speed. As the torpedo entered the water the boat quickly turned out of its way and retreated.

Although the CMBs did account for the sinking of a German destroyer as well as a few other minor vessels, they were specialized craft designed to perform the specific task of an acute and short-ranged attack on a known target under calm sea conditions. They did not have the endurance to accomplish longer search and attack missions such as were required in World War Two when targets of opportunity were scouted over much longer patrol periods and much larger areas.

A number of German boat yards were employed in the design and building of high-speed torpedo boats. Unlike their British counterparts, the German Navy specified boats capable of good performance even in heavy seas. The result was typically a semi-displacement type hull with a round bilge. Somewhat heavier and longer than their British counterparts, this semiplaning hull would become the trademark of German torpedo boats through World War One right up to the present. Of wooden construction and most notably a product of the Lürssen yard, the boats were powered by gasoline engines originally intended for use in the Zeppelin airships and converted for marine use. At 56 ft in length, these boats with their three engines could make over 30 knots. Unfortunately, they were not aggressively employed by the German Naval High Command and were used more often in the destruction of anti U-boat mine nets. Nonetheless, they were the immediate forerunners of the famous and highly successful *Schnellbooten* (also known as S-Boats or E-Boats) of World War Two.

The most successful use of motor torpedo boats during World War One was unquestionably made by the Royal Italian Navy against the Austrians. The Italian speedboats were powered by the excellent Isotta Fraschini engines, variations of which would later be purchased by the British for their motor torpedo boats (MTBs). The Italian craft were known as MAS boats and numbered something of the order of 350 at the end of the war. The sinking of the Austrian battleship *Wein* by two of these boats during the war served notice to traditionalist admirals the world around that the motor torpedo boats had arrived as a weapon to be dealt with.

One other notable World War One program must be mentioned here. When the war broke out, the British impressed hundreds of private yachts and motor boats into the naval reserves. In the first year of the war these former pleasure craft performed yeoman service, indeed invaluable service, to the navy: picket duties, harbor patrol, transport, anti-submarine patrol, rescue – all vital tasks which the Royal Navy had scarce resources to fulfill.

Top

The British Coastal Motor Boats (CMBs) of World War 1 were a direct application of the *Miranda* **and** *Maple Leaf* **single step hydroplane racers of 1912. Capable of between 35 to 40 knots depending on engine combinations, the CMBs were never really given much of a chance to prove themselves thanks to traditional conservative thinking on behalf of the Royal Navy heirarchy.**

Bottom

In the later stages of the war, Thornycroft began production of a twin-engine 55-foot CMB pictured here. Although wholly unsuited for anti-submarine work, some of the boats were fitted with depth charges—as was this example. Many of the boats ended up being used as fast minelayers, a rather unspectacular employment for such hybrid craft.

Left
The lineage of World War Two PT-Boats can be traced all the way back to the 1870s with such craft as Thornycroft's 84 ft steam-powered torpedo boat *Lightning*. Redesignated TB-1, she was the first torpedo boat to enter service with the Royal Navy with the intent that she would carry the Whitehead torpedo in offensive operations against enemy ships. She was soon relegated, however, to coastal defensive operations, for although she could make 18 knots with a full load, her range was quite limited as she could steam for only about three hours at high speed.

Bottom
In a photo which nicely illustrates the manner in which the British CMB carried its torpedo, a 40 foot boat operating in the Caspian Sea against Bolshevik shipping during 1919 as part of the half-hearted Allied attempt to stem the tide against the revolutionaries. The possibility of running afoul of one's own torpedo left something to be desired in the over-the-stern launching system.

The legendary Commodore Garfield Wood is seen here behind the wheel of his last and most powerful British International Trophy defender, *Miss America X*. This single-step thirty-eight foot hydroplane boasted a total of 6,400 hp from four supercharged Packard engines driving two propellers in tandem. Seated beside Wood is his mechanic Orlin Johnson.

Within a short time these former private craft were all but spent in terms of their ability to withstand the day-in, day-out abuse to which they were subjected. British yards were busy with trawler and other larger naval construction projects so, in search of a solution to the requirement for a fleet of general-purpose motor boats, the Admiralty contacted the Elco Boat Company of Bayonne, New Jersey. By April 1915 Elco had secured a contract from the Royal Navy to build fifty wooden-hulled motorboats. It was the Admiralty's intention to equip these 75 ft craft for a primary role as anti-submarine boats. They would, of course, perform other duties as well. The resultant Elco design with its round-bilged displacement hull was by no means a speedboat with its top speed of 19 knots – and they tended to roll something awful in a sea – but they were tough, seaworthy little craft. Elco, under the leadership of Henry Sutphen, obtained manufacturing facilities in Canada to ease their way around the neutrality problem. These facilities had

to be greatly expanded when the Royal Navy ordered an additional 500 boats, this time to an enlarged 80 ft design. The only possible way Elco could fulfill its contracts would be to mass-produce the boats on an assembly line from entirely prefabricated components, and this is exactly what was done. The building program was a resounding success both for the British and for Elco, who developed invaluable experience in the mass production via prefabrication business of making relatively large wooden motor boats. It would be an ability put to great advantage in World War Two.

BETWEEN THE WARS

When World War One ended, Elco went back into the business of building pleasure boats. Throughout the 1920s German and Italian official interest in motor torpedo boats remained fairly active, the respective governments sponsoring at least *some* de-

velopmental projects as well as a continuation of the bank of operational experience gained during the war.

In Great Britain and the United States, however, official interest in fast torpedo boats soon died away almost entirely. The navies of these two countries, with but a few exceptions, spent their money on capital ship development. Once again it fell to the private-venture boat yards and the well-heeled patrons of racing to continue the advancement of motor boat technology. In England Thornycroft and Vosper really did not suffer horribly for the Royal Navy's lack of support. They were able to to sell many motor torpedo boats to smaller foreign navies including those of Siam, Japan, China, Spain, Sweden, the Netherlands, Greece and Finland. These boats were, however, based on British CMB hydroplane designs of World War One and as such did not represent a great deal in the advancement of the torpedo boat concept.

It was the continual pressure of racing competition that finally brought the stepless planing hull into widespread use in speed-boat design. The concave bow section smoothing to a virtually flat stern is commonplace even today, but such a design was quite an innovation, and certainly a departure from what had gone before, for the racers of the 1920s. While the stepless mono hull is inherently more stable and more maneuverable than the hydroplane (at any speed), it also has a greater wetted surface area which thus requires more power to achieve the same speeds as a like-sized hydroplane. It was the development of relatively light-weight, very powerful engines that brought the stepless hull to the fore for possible naval applications during the 1930s, although the single-step hydroplane continued to dominate the realm of unlimited class racing where all-out speed on calm waters dictated their continued use.

On the American side much of the credit for engine and hull development goes to Commodore Garfield Wood, the wealthy industrialist who early on realized that the

Miss America X at speed during 1933, the last year in which Gar Wood defended his BI Trophy. This boat held the world's water speed record at 108.4 knots. The substantial developmental work that went into the perfection of the Packard marine engines used in Wood's *Miss America* series boats would be invaluable in the production of PT-Boats to come a few years later.

marinization of high-powered aviation engines was the ticket to success. With his series of *Miss America* hydroplanes powered by Wood-modified marine versions of the famous Packard-built Liberty aircraft engine, Gar Wood managed to dominate the competition for the British International Trophy throughout most of the 1920s. By 1928 Wood was building hydroplanes with 1,000 hp Packard engines, capable of 90 mph. It was also in this year that Wood would meet his nemesis, Hubert Scott-Paine, an Englishman who would be instrumental in forming the first American PT-Boat program a decade later.

Scott-Paine was a blustery character of many talents, not at all an example of the so-called typical British reserve. After hiring on in 1916 this man had worked his way up to the position of director and then owner of Supermarine Aviation within four years. In 1922 he built the winning aircraft in the Schneider Trophy Race. One year later he sold his interest in Supermarine to become one of the central figures in the founding of British Airways. Not only was Scott-Paine an innovative designer (although never formally schooled in engineering), he was also a skilled and resourceful project manager. What is more, he had a genuine feel for public relations and was a super salesman to both government and private sectors. By 1927 Scott-Paine had turned his attentions to boat building. He established the British Power Boat Company near Southampton with an eye toward mass-producing pleasure motor boats in an operation similar to that set up by the successful Chris Craft Corporation in America. In 1928 Scott-Paine was asked by the famous land speed record-holder Sir Henry Segrave to design and build a boat with which he could beat Gar Wood and return the absolute water speed record once again to England. Scott-Paine accepted the proposition as a great means of promoting the British Power Boat Company name. The resultant boat, *Miss England*, a 28 ft single-step hydroplane, did indeed beat Wood's

Gar Wood not only built unlimited class world record holders but also designed and built entries in other motorboat classes as well. This early 1930s photograph shows the Gar, Jr winning the twenty-mile race for express cruisers at Miami, Florida. Overhead is the Aero Limited Mark 4 in the process of winning a concurrent seaplane race flown over the same course as that followed by the motorboats. This was a great publicity shot for Packard as both seaplane and boat were powered by 400 hp Liberty engines.

Miss America VII in 1929, although the two boats never raced for the British International Trophy which Wood retained. Fierce competition continued on through the 1920s between a series of Wood's *Miss America* boats and various English entries, culminating in Wood's last defense of the Trophy in 1933. By this time, Wood had become very closely associated with Packard and in fact had invested thousands of his own dollars in that company's efforts at supercharging and further developing the marine version of the Liberty engine. By 1932 Wood was campaigning the monstrous *Miss America X*, a 38 ft hydroplane powered by no fewer than four 1,600 hp Packards. He was challenged in 1933 by Scott-Paine again, the redoubtable Englishman this time showing up with a 24 ft all-aluminium hydroplane dubbed *Miss Britain III*. Unfortunately, Scott-Paine was unable to obtain examples of the powerful Rolls-Royce Merlin engine due to their allocation for aircraft production. Using instead a single 1,400 hp Napier Lion, Scott-Paine could not match *Miss America X*'s straight-away speeds of over 100 knots, but his boat was considerably more

maneuverable through the turns, and he managed to give Wood one of the closest and most exciting races on record.

While all of this racing activity took place, the British and American navies paid little official attention to the idea of an offensive motor boat force. Curiously enough, however, countries such as Germany, Italy and France, where racing was not nearly so extensive, initiated important naval programs resulting in fast torpedo boat flotillas by the mid 1930s.

The true lineage of the United States PT-Boat of World War Two can be traced to a series of craft built by Scott-Paine for the British Air Force beginning in 1935. The wily designer created a fine boat and then convinced the RAF that they could not do without it for such work as crash rescue and tender duty around seaplane bases. Scott-Paine's finest example of the air-sea rescue boat was a hard-chine stepless design of 64 ft equipped with three 500 hp Napier Sea Lion engines. Twenty-two of the craft were built over a five-year period and proved themselves highly successful. The stepless hulls were vastly easier to construct than the

During the 1920s the prohibition of liquor spawned a virtual armada of small fast 'rum runners', with whom a beefed up United States Coast Guard did constant battle. It has long been rumored that a number of the original PT-Boat's enlisted men, particularly the mechanics, cut their teeth on high-powered rum-running boats which operated heavily off the east coast of the United States. Note the bullet holes in the port side window of this fast 60-footer named *Diatome*, as she appeared at the time of her capture.

stepped hydroplane boats (a very important consideration in wartime construction) and offered the distinct advantage of better rough-water performance and maneuverability over a stepped design. The multilayered, diagonally planked mahogony hulls were strong, yet light enough to allow the boats to make a best speed of 40 knots. But perhaps the most important result of the crash boat program was the crafts' demonstrated ability to stay at sea for extended periods with a cruising range of over 800 miles. When this factor was combined with the impressive dash capability and attractive load-carrying potential of the 64-foot hull, the conclusions were so obvious that even the Royal Navy could not ignore them much longer. In contrast, things were still dormant on the other side of the Atlantic in 1935.

A torpedo carrying version of Scott-Paine's crash boat soon met with Admiralty approval, and by 1936 the Royal Navy owned six such boats. Increased loading brought the maximum dash speed down to 33 knots. What is more, the boats were equipped with a rather curious and wholly inefficient means for dispatching the two 18 in torpedoes carried by each craft. The routine went something as follows: As a boat approached a target, speed was reduced to allow two lattice-work racks, each about nine feet long,

to be flipped over and extended out over the stern. The boat then moved in on the target and, when within range, would slow briefly and then accelerate as quickly as possible. This sudden forward motion caused the two torpedoes, suspended on overhead rails in the engine room, to slide backward out of two large portals in the stern. As they exited, the torpedoes were held straight by the extended lattice railing until they cleared the portals, and then fell into the water. The boat then had to turn quickly away to avoid being struck by its own torpedoes. It was an excellent lesson in how not to launch torpedoes from small boats.

Eighteen of these craft were eventually built before the war, equipping three squadrons of 'MTBs', as the boats soon became known. For obvious reasons, these craft would not see much in the way of operational use during the coming war.

Even while production of the 60 ft MTBs continued (the air-sea rescue hull had been shortened 4 ft on the MTBs) it was realized that a new and improved design was called for. Scott-Paine's answer was a 70 ft boat built in 1938 and powered by three 1,000 hp Rolls-Royce Merlin engines. These engines were marvellous powerplants, but were not being produced fast enough to allow their use in anything other than aircraft. The new

design, however, was a good one. The 70-footer could carry four 18 in torpedoes in forward launching tubes and deliver them at speeds approaching 44 knots. It was an improvement over the 60 ft design in virtually every other category as well, including construction, seaworthiness and crew accommodations.

Unfortunately, after all of his pioneering work and eventual success in finally getting the Royal Navy interested in MTBs, Scott-Paine's 70-footer was voted into second place by the Admiralty in favor of a Vosper design, basic permutations of which would be the Royal Navy's primary MTB type throughout World War Two. Scott-Paine was given an order that amounted to little more than a pat on the head. In addition to purchasing his 70 ft prototype, the Royal Navy agreed to purchase nine production boats. The decision was as much political as anything else, a big stink having been raised by certain quarters concerning alleged underhand dealing by Scott-Paine and the seeming favoritism which the Navy had shown toward the British Power Boat Company in the past. The result was that Scott-Paine was left waiting on the church steps – but not for long.

These events would have a profound effect on the other side of the Atlantic.

An excellent view of PT-32 at speed in her pre-war paint. As a member of the original Squadron 3 based in the Philippines at the start of the war, this 77-foot Elco boat managed to slip a torpedo into what was believed to be a Japanese cruiser which had taken the tiny boat under fire off Bataan, this on the night of 1 February, 1942. The boat was one of the four that remained operational in the squadron long enough to evacuate the MacArthur party from the islands on March 11, although PT-32 never completed the trip. Due to her thoroughly deteriorated condition, she had to be abandoned and destroyed enroute.

2

The First American Boats

Were it not for the efforts of a few visionary men – including the President – who virtually had to jam the concept of small torpedo-carrying boats down the throats of some of the U.S. Navy hierarchy, there may never have been an American PT-Boat force as it came to exist in World War Two.

By 1936 scattered individuals within the hierarchy of the United States Navy had become aware of the importance of foreign developments regarding motor torpedo boats and began, of their own initiative, to examine the potential worth of such craft to their own service. In December 1936 Rear Admiral Emory S. Land, Chief of the Navy's Bureau of Construction and Repair, penned a note to the Chief of Naval Operations, Admiral Leahy, pointing out the fact that much had taken place in the way of torpedo boat development since the CMBs of World War One and that a force of such craft might be of some use to the United States Navy. His argument followed the reasoning that the boats could be used as a defensive or deterrent force in the protection of coastal areas, thus allowing larger ships to be released for offensive strike operations.

Leahy passed the letter on to the Secretary of the Navy, who in turn sent it on to the Navy's General Board for review. The General Board concluded that while the current usefulness of such craft in peacetime might be very limited, given America's geographical makeup, '. . . future situations can occur under which it would be possible for such small craft to be used on directly offensive missions – as is no doubt contemplated in certain foreign navies.' The Board recommended a modest de-velopmental program be initiated. Secretary of the Navy Claud Swanson endorsed the Board's recommendations on 7 May 1937.

There is evidence to suggest that the Board may have reached its decision thanks at least in part to the efforts of a man for whom the entire program would later prove quite valuable. Former Army Chief of Staff General Douglas MacArthur was commander of the United States forces in the Philippines in 1937. He correctly evaluated the serious

Although something less than perfect from a photographic standpoint, this is an extremely rare aerial view of PT-9 – the original Scott-Paine boat sold to Elco – firing all four of its torpedoes at the same time.

weaknesses in the defenses of those islands in light of Japanese expansionism. He reasoned that while he did not have the power to convince Washington that additional capital ships were needed immediately in the area, he might be able to convince the powers-that-be to supply him with the next best thing in terms of an increased naval fighting force. A flotilla of fast torpedo boats would be perfectly suited for operations among the Philippine Islands, and he felt that ninety such boats would be sufficient to do the job. While in the United States in early 1937 the General presented his arguments to a number of Naval officials, but had little luck until finally calling upon his friend, Chief of Naval Operations Admiral Leahy. Leahy then allowed MacArthur to present his suggestions to the Board. The General's actions were a credit to his farsightedness.

Assistant Secretary of the Navy Charles Edison was an early champion of the torpedo boat cause, as was in fact the President of the United States himself. Fully one year after Secretary Swanson approved the Board's recommendation, Congress appropriated a supplement to the 1938 Fiscal Year Naval Program '. . . for the construction of experimental vessels, none of which shall exceed 3,000 tons standard displacement.' The sum of $15,000,000 was earmarked for the program and was to be spent at the discretion of the President of the United States, a testiment to Roosevelt's personal interest in the program. As Assistant Secretary of the Navy in World War One, Roosevelt had become convinced of the value of the British CMBs, although he realized they had never been given the opportunity to achieve their full potential. It was, in fact, the weight of the President's backing that insured the $15 million Congressional appropriation.

Within days of the Congressional action, plans were afoot within the Navy to sponsor a design contest for small craft, specifications for which included a 54 ft and 70 ft motor torpedo boat. The smaller boat was to have a minimum top speed of 40 knots with a radius of 240 miles at cruising speed. Armament specified was to be two torpedoes only, with an alternative arrangement of machine-guns and depth charges. One last qualification was that the craft was not to exceed twenty tons in weight. This was to allow the craft to remain within easy lifting capacity of boom-equipped cargo ships for quick transport overseas.

The armament specifications for the 70 ft design were naturally more substantial. At least two 21 in. torpedoes would be carried in addition to depth charges and anti-aircraft guns. This boat, too, would have a minimum top speed of 40 knots with a 550 mile cruising range.

30 September 1938 was the deadline for submission of proposals, and by that date the Navy had some thirty-seven suggested designs in hand. The Navy picked three of the designs as promising in the 54 ft category and five for further consideration in the 70 ft group. The heavy initial turnout was due in no small part to the reward of $15,000 to be given to the originator of the winning designs in each class.

With the field narrowed down, the eight finalists were now asked to submit more detailed plans for their boats, to be in Navy hands no later than 7 November 1938. After intense review, the Navy announced five months later, on 21 March 1939, that Professor George Crouch was the winner in the 54 ft class while the naval architectural firm of Sparkman and Stephens had taken top honors in the 70 ft category. Two months later the Navy announced the awarding of contracts to three boat yards for construction of six experimental boats based on these

Left
PT-1 is seen here being transported aboard the seaplane tender USS *Pocomoke* during April 1942. PTs 1 and 2 were built by the Miami Shipbuilding Company but it would be nearly two and a half years from the time they were contracted in mid-1939 before they were delivered to the Navy. The two completed boats spent the better part of two years sitting in their builder's yard awaiting the installation of their twin 1,200 hp Vimalert engines. By November 1941 the engines were finally installed and the boats delivered to the Navy, but by that time it had long since been learned that bigger boats were needed for service, and the two 58 ft boats were considered too obsolete even to enter service with the Melville training squadron. As such, on 24 December 1941, PTs 1 and 2 were reclassified as small boats and spent the rest of their days performing menial tasks along the eastern seaboard.

Right
Initial American efforts at designing and building PT-Boats left a good deal to be desired. PT-3, shown here underway, was built – along with her twin sister PT-4 – by the Fisher Boat Works of Detroit, Michigan. Based on Professor Crouch's winning entry in the Navy-sponsored design contest of 1938, the Bureau of Ships tinkered with the drawings somewhat before construction began. This 58 ft boat was designed to a specification that called for the boat to be small and light enough to be lifted by crane on to a mother warship or 'PT carrier'. The concept was never worked out in anything other than theory, and it was soon learned that a boat 58 feet long was too small to be of any real use. During April 1941 PTs 3 and 4 were handed over to Great Britain on lend-lease, where they went on to serve as MTBs 273 and 274.

Right

After being purchased from the British Power Boat Company by Elco's Henry Sutphen, PT-9 was shipped to New York on the deck of the SS *President Roosevelt*, from which the boat is seen here being unloaded upon arrival in September 1939. PT-9 would be the ancestor of all Elco-built PT-Boats to see service during World War Two.

Bottom

After arrival in the United States PT-9 was put through her paces for virtually anyone who would watch by none other than the designer himself, Hubert Scott-Paine, seen at the controls in this photograph during a demonstration run off Groton, Connecticut. Note that the boat is still fitted with tubes sized for launching the British 18 in. torpedo.

winning designs. By this time, the navy had adopted the term of 'Patrol-Torpedo Boat' in reference to their soon to be acquired craft, and as such each of the boats was assigned a 'PT' number. For ever more, American motor torpedo boats would be known as 'PT-Boats'.

Appropriately enough the first boats were assigned the numbers 1 through 6. PTs 1 and 2, based on Professor Crouch's design, were contracted to the Miami Shipbuilding Company. PTs 3 and 4, also based on Crouch's hull lines but tinkered with considerably by the Bureau of Ships, were contracted to the Fisher Boat Works of Detroit, Michigan. PTs 5 and 6 were to be based on the Sparkman and Stephens design although, again due to Bureau of Ships modifications, the boats were to be stretched from 70 to 81 feet in length. The contracts for these two boats were let to Higgins Industries Incorporated of New Orleans. The Higgins company was eminently qualified to build such small craft. Founded originally as the Higgins Lumber and Export Company by Andrew Jackson Higgins, a ship repair yard was later established that soon grew into a full-fledged boat-building business. By 1937 the name Higgins was well known for rugged shallow water workboats. Higgins would come to play an important role in the production of PT-Boats in World War Two, but certainly not by virtue of the Sparkman and Stephens design. The three contracts were all awarded during May and June 1939 and along with these first six boats construction was also authorized for two wholly Navy designs that had been produced by the Bureau of Ships. PTs 7 and

8, both boats of 81 ft would be built by the government in the Philadelphia Navy Yard. Clearly the Navy was going about this research and development business in the best and most thorough manner it could. Time would soon become a big factor in the program, however, for the beginning of war in Europe was only three months away.

While the Navy was busily engaged in design contests, other events were taking place that would have profound effects on the United States PT-Boat program. The Elco Naval Division of the Electric Boat Company has already been mentioned, particularly with regard to their construction of hundreds of 80 ft motor patrol boats for the British during World War One. In 1938 the Electric Boat Company was approaching its 50th anniversary of operation. The company had its beginnings in 1892, when it was founded for the specific purpose of building fifty-five 36 ft electric launches for use on the lagoons at the Chicago World's Fair. This was the beginning of a long success story frequently characterized by innovative thinking on the part of employees. Elco built *Hurrion*, the first oil-electric yacht; it built the Auto-Boat, the first high-speed runabout. For the United States Life Saving Service Elco designed and built the first self-righting, self-bailing, non-sinkable power lifeboat, and in 1911 the company constructed *Idealia*, the first Diesel Motor Yacht. But perhaps most noteworthy in the Elco history was the 1914 introduction of the 32 ft double-cabin Elco Cruisette, for it represented the first practical use of the standardized construction principles that would be essential in two world wars when

PTs 7 and 8 were 81 ft boats designed and built by the United States Navy in Philadelphia. PT-7 was of wooden construction and was powered by four Hall-Scott engines coupled to two shafts. PT-8, pictured here, featured all-aluminium construction and was powered by four 1,000 hp Allison V-12s arranged as two X-engines. They were drag-started at 15 knots by a single 550 hp Hall-Scott engine which was also used for backing. As a result of heavy construction techniques and fittings, PT-7 and PT-8 were slower than planned and, thanks in part to frequent breakdowns, were never considered very satisfactory. PT-7 was handed over to the British during April 1941 on lend-lease, but PT-8 remained with the United States Navy after being reclassified as YP-110 in October 1941. The boat survived the war in a remarkably well preserved condition, thanks to her aluminium hull, and was used for additional developmental testing after the war.

Top and Center Left
Two fine studies of the first United States-built example of Hubert Scott-Paine's 70 ft design turning up top speed in the calm waters of New York Harbor during late 1940. PT-10 is painted in the peacetime light gray applied to all the first production boats. Although calm water performance was outstanding, service tests soon revealed structural weaknesses that were remedied in the soon-to-come 77-footers.

Bottom Left
The boat that started it all for the United States Navy, British Power Boat's PT-9, leads two of her American-built sisters past the Statue of Liberty during December 1940, shortly after the delivery of the boats to the Navy. Within five months these three 70-footers would be back in British hands.

Bottom
A fine study of eight of the ten 70-footers of the original Squadron 2. This photo was taken during January 1941 just as the boats were preparing to depart New England for a test deployment to Florida and the Caribbean. Upon their return all the boats seen here would be transferred to Great Britain.

mass production from pre-assembled components – some manufactured by sub-contractors in other parts of the country – would be the only way to achieve the kinds of production orders being taken.

Mr Henry R. Sutphen was one of the first Elco employees, joining the firm as a young man in the year of its founding. By World War One, Sutphen had risen to a place of prominence in the company and was responsible for the conception of the already mentioned wooden motor boats built for the British during that war. By 1938 Sutphen was the executive vice-president of a multi-division corporation. The Electric Boat Company not only operated the Elco Naval Division in Bayonne, New Jersey, but was now building submarines for the United States Navy at their new submarine works in Groton, Connecticut. Needless to say this was a program of extreme importance for the United States Navy in 1938. The third division was the Electro-Dynamic Works,

responsible for much of the auxiliary electrical equipment used on US Navy capital ships of the time. In January 1939, aboard a brand-new destroyer which was making a trial run out of the shipyards at Kearny, New Jersey, Assistant Secretary of the Navy Charles Edison, soon to become Secretary upon Swanson's death and aboard for the test run, cornered one of the other invited guests just as the new DD passed the Elco plant at Bayonne. The guest was Elco's Henry Sutphen, and what Edison wanted to talk to him about was the possibility of getting Elco interested in entering the PT-Boat field.

Edison was aware that boats were being constructed in England which were, in all likelihood, already superior in performance to the first American boats still at least a year away from completion. He made the suggestion to the Board that obtaining one of these boats might be a wise move and that he knew where a 70 ft example might be obtained. With an air of understatement, the

Board concluded that, 'Inasmuch as said design is known to be the result of several years' development, the General Board considers it highly advisable that such craft be obtained as a check on our own development.' With the President's approval, Edison had $5 million of his original $15 million left and he was determined to use it to best advantage. This is where Sutphen and Elco came into the picture. It would have been imprudent for the United States Navy to send official representatives to England to return with British-built merchandise. Such a move might well have caused an uproar among other United States boat-building yards as well as among elements of organized labor, all fearing that the Navy was contemplating spending money overseas that should, in fact, be spent at home – or so the argument went. Edison neatly sidestepped this problem when he suggested to Sutphen that he should travel to England – at his own expense – to investigate the various boats and try to purchase one – at his own expense – with an eye toward licensed manufacture in the United States. Without any sort of written agreement, Sutphen sailed for England along with his chief engineer Irwin Chase, on 10 February 1939, having no more than an understanding with Edison that he would do everything he could to convince the Navy to purchase the boat once it was in the United States.

Edison could not have chosen a better man for the task at hand. Sutphen was well respected by the Admiralty thanks to his tremendous efforts on their behalf during World War One. Once in England, Sutphen was given the utmost in official cooperation. Although he inspected all of the other facilities then engaged in the manufacture of torpedo boats, it was with Scott-Paine's British Powerboat design that Sutphen was most impressed. The two Americans were taken with the sleek-lined boat's high speed and maneuverability. This was the same 70 ft boat which the Admiralty had declined to purchase in anything other than trifling numbers in favor of the Vosper design.

With the blessing of the Admiralty Sutphen made a deal with Scott-Paine for the purchase of one boat complete with three Rolls-Royce Merlin engines and the rights to manufacture the craft in the United States. Sutphen then immediately wired the news of his purchase to the Navy, who passed the information along to Roosevelt himself. The President gave his blessing to the scheme and Elco was in business.

It was not until September 1939 that Scott-Paine's 70-footer arrived in New York, carried on the deck of the SS *President*

A bow-on view of PT-15, an Elco 70-footer, before being handed over to the British. This angle emphasizes the high freeboard and shallow 'V' of this design.

Roosevelt. On the day it arrived, World War Two was two days old. The boat, now designated PT-9, was hauled by barge to the Electric Boat Company's facility at Groton, Connecticut, where trials were begun. So intent upon seeing his design be proven a success was Scott-Paine that the ex-racer put the boat through its paces himself. The boat impressed everyone with its durability and high speed. With only two of the eight planned United States boats under construction, Edison felt confident in recommending to the President that the remaining $5 million should be spent on an actual production order to be placed with the Elco for as many 70 ft boats of the Scott-Paine design as could be had. Sutphen estimated that he could build about sixteen boats for the amount, but he was again prevailed upon by Edison, by now Acting Secretary of the Navy, to build twenty-three boats, just the number needed to equip two complete squadrons of twelve each. Sutphen later

maintained that this first deal cost him $600,000 in losses, but Elco would have more than enough in the way of PT-Boat orders exactly two years to the day after the signing of this first contract on 7 December 1939.

Even as the wheels of production began to turn, it would be more than six months before the Navy would take official delivery of its first boat, PT-9, on 17 June 1940. This was largely due to the fact that Elco engineers used this first boat as a template to duplicate every part needed to reproduce the boat. Apparently Scott-Paine had kept something less than accurate blue-print records during the prototype boat's construction period.

One month before the Navy took possession of PT-9 an official organizational system was worked out whereby three squadrons would be put into service initially. The first squadron, Squadron 1, would be composed of all the experimental boats then under construction. Squadron 2 would be an all-Elco squadron consisting of PT-9 through 20, while Squadron 3 would consist of Elco 70-footers equipped with depth charges and other anti-submarine gear to be designated PTCs 1 through 12.

Squadron 1 was finally commissioned on 24 July 1940 with but three boats available for service. PT-9 was on hand with the intention that she would be transferred to Squadron 2 when that group commissioned. PTs 3 and 4 had also been delivered late the month before, these being the Crouch-designed boats built by Fisher. These two boats were equipped with Packard engines like those that were to be used in all Elco boats in place of the Rolls-Royce units in PT-9. As far as the remaining American experimental boats were concerned, PTs 1 and 2 never did join Squadron 1. The boats sat in the yard of their builder for a year and a half awaiting installation of their 1,200 hp Vimalert engines. PT-5, one of the boats awarded to Higgins, also went wanting for lack of its Vimalert engines, although it was eventually delivered to the Navy only to be proven

lacking in performance. The other Higgins-built boat, PT-6, was never taken over by the Navy as it was completed long after other Navy programs had superseded it, the boat eventually being sold to Finland. As far as the Navy-built PTs 7 and 8 were concerned, their performance, too, was wholly unsatisfactory. As it turned out the boats were considerably heavier than the design called for, and performance suffered measurably. It should be noted, however, that one of the boats, PT-8, was constructed with an aluminium hull which, even in the face of utter neglect, survived the war in excellent condition to be used as a test bed for continuing research.

By 1 January 1941 Squadrons 1 and 2 were worked up to the point where a test deployment to Cuba was ordered via Miami Beach. Squadron 2 was almost fully equipped with boats but Squadron 1 had only PTs 3, 4, 7 and 8 in service. The operational experience gained during this first and, to a certain extent, abortive deployment was invaluable to future PT programs. The boats of Squadron 1 failed miserably, and Squadron 2's Elcos did not go without mishap either. In one case an Elco boat suffered a separation of

the deck from the sides at the gunwale approximately a quarter of the length from the bow. This was corrected by installing molded plywood angles to take care of longitudinal shear. It was also learned that while proceeding near top speed through waves of a certain height and length bottom frames would crack in the pounding area forward. Frames were strengthened and additional frames interspersed. But it should be noted that these failures were just what the Navy was hoping for as they provided a means of working out serious bugs before the boats would experience service as combat units.

Upon the return of the two squadrons to New York all of the 70 ft Elcos, along with PTs 3, 4, 5 and 7, were earmarked for turnover to the British under the lend-lease program. The loss of the first batch of Elcos to the British was largely overshadowed by the promised delivery of a new and improved version of the Scott-Paine design. PT-20 – the last boat on the original Elco contract –

A group of the original Elco 70-footers running abreast off the east coast shortly after the commissioning of Squadron 2 in late 1940.

Top Left
After their test deployment to the Caribbean during the winter of 1941, the 70-footers of the original Squadron 2 were handed over to Great Britain. Shipped to England, the boats were immediately modified with British equipment and renumbered. The former PT-14 is seen here in British service, renumbered as MTB-263 and equipped with two permanently angled British-type torpedo tubes as well as two .30 caliber Lewis machine-guns on the bow. This boat survived the war to be sold into civilian hands in 1946.

Center Left
PT-20 was originally intended to be the last boat on the original Elco production order for 70 ft boats. As the need for a bigger boat crystalized during early operations it was decided to make PT-20 the first of a new type. Essentially what was done was to add seven feet to the stern of the 70 ft design, although there were subtle differences in hull lines and PT-20 was launched on 14 March 1941 as the first of a total of forty-nine 77 ft boats built for the United States Navy and Great Britain.

Bottom Left
Hubert Scott-Paine's British Power Boat Company was not totally shut out by Vosper, landing a small contract for the production of their 70-foot design for the Royal Navy. One such boat, MGB-64, is seen here, the photo clearly demonstrating the British-built superstructure arrangement for their motor gunboat configuration. These craft were intended to counter German E-Boat raids on coastal convoys, a mission for which torpedoes would be useless.

Top Right
The 70 ft PT-12, seen here passing the Manhattan skyline as she heads out of New York Harbor, was delivered to the Navy and placed in service on 14 November 1940 as part of the original Elco contract.

Center Right
A batch of Elco 77-footers, PTs 49 through 58, were redesignated before completion as BPTs (British Patrol Torpedo) 1 through 10, and were handed over to Great Britain during February and March 1942. The balance of this group of boats are visible in this photograph, taken off the New Jersey coast, just before they were handed over. The boats in this photograph still bear their BPT number designations – the boat in the foreground is BPT-8 – and are being operated by American crews. Once in British hands the boats were renumbered as MTBs 307 through 316 and were sent to the Mediterranean, where several were lost due to enemy action at Tobruk during September 1942.

Bottom Right
PT-17, one of the original Elco 70 ft boats, is seen here at speed off New York Harbor during March 1942. Four months later, on 11 July 1941, she would be handed over to the British under lend-lease to serve in the English Channel as MTB-266, where she would be lost in April 1944. The mosquito and torpedo emblem on the cabin side is clearly visible in this photo, and it is easy to see why these emblems were removed once the boats reached the combat zones.

Top Left

After his rather bad experience in trying to build PT-6 from the Sparkman and Stephens design, Andrew Jackson Higgins designed and built his own private venture boat to compete in the 'Plywood Derbies'. This experimental 76 ft boat was given the designation PT-70 by the Navy and proved to be highly acceptable, with many of the officers and men who had the opportunity to test-ride the boat indicating they felt it was superior to the Elco 77-footer. With its good performance in the Derbies PT-70 earned a production contract for Higgins Industries, although the design was altered to increase the length slightly to 78 feet. PT-70 was retained by the Navy but, as an experimental boat, it was never placed in squadron service. The boat was reclassified as a district patrol vessel, YP-107, on 24 September 1942.

Bottom Left

Bow-on view of the Huckins-built PT-95 off Jacksonville. This design was found to have some serious handling problems and that is one of the reasons why the Huckins boats were never placed in mass production. They possessed a wide transom which caused the boats to yaw excessively in a following sea. What is more, while proceeding in echelon the following boat had a tendency to fall off the bow wave of the boat ahead, instead of cutting through it, causing the helmsman to lose control. Other serious structural deficiencies were found in the boats as well.

Top and Bottom Right

PT-95 was the first Huckins production boat delivered to the Navy. The boat is seen here running at high speed during manufacturer's trials near the Huckins plant off Jacksonville, Florida. The photographs were taken on 14 July 1942, nine days before the boat was officially handed over to the Navy. Powered by four Packard engines, only a few more examples of this 78 ft boat would be built by Huckins, the Navy having finally decided to standardize on the Higgins and Elco types. PT-95 and the next two boats in line, PTs 96 and 97, were sent to join Squadron 4 at Melville, Rhode Island, where they were used to train PT sailors and officers for the duration of the war. The next five Huckins boats, PTs 98 through 102, became elements of Squadron 14, which was assigned in early 1943 to guard the Panama Sea Frontier. Ten more Huckins boats were completed and were collectively commissioned into Squadron 26 in March 1943. They were then shipped to the Hawaiian Islands and, like their sisters in Panama, were charged with the responsibility of patrolling the Hawaiian Sea Frontier. Neither of these squadrons ever made contact with the enemy.

was being completed with an additional seven-foot section added to the stern to bring the overall length to 77 ft. The Navy had requested this modification, even as Squadron 2 was receiving the last of its 70-footers, as it had been determined desirable for all future PTs to be able to carry four 21 in. torpedoes. This was too great a load for the 70-footers, and the requirement resulted in the modification of the design. These new 77 ft PT-Boats would be the first to experience combat in the service of the United States Navy. The boats of Squadron 3, those craft which had been equipped as fast submarine chasers, were also eventually leased to the British, where they began distinguished careers as gunboats in the British Coastal Forces.

As a result of the test deployment to Florida during the winter of 1940–41, a great deal of operational information was gathered, but opinions at all levels of the naval command with regard to which types of boats offered the most promise seemed to take off in all directions. It was clear that the time had come for some sort of determination to be made about which would be the boat designs chosen for the new construction programs that would begin as part of a $50 million appropriation for fiscal year 1941. Accordingly the Navy Board of Inspection and Survey decided to conduct comparative service tests among a number of second-generation boats then under construction. The plan was conceived during May 1941, and the first competition was held during the following July. As a result of one of the contractors protesting that his boat had not received a fair evaluation in the first test, a second trial was run during August. The participating vessels were rated on structural efficiency, habitability, access, arrangement for adequate control, communications facilities, tactical diameters, seakeeping qualities, maximum sustained speed, maneuverability and standardization. Part of the competition involved a 190 mile run, which quickly broke down into a race on both occasions it was administered, starting from New London, Connecticut; around Block Island; out to and around the Fire Island Light Ship; thence around the Montauk Point Whistling Buoy, and back to New London. The races were unofficially dubbed 'The Plywood Derbys'.

By the time the competition dates rolled around, several examples of the Elco 77 ft boats had been completed and were entered. But there were other serious contenders on hand as well. After a bad experience with the Sparkman-Stephens design while trying to convert it to the actual working prototype

embodied in PT-6, Andrew Higgins, using his own finances, built a boat of his own design with the understanding that the Navy would purchase the craft if it was found to be satisfactory. This independent Higgins design was represented in the competition by PT-70. This boat was 76 ft long, was powered by three Packard engines just like those used in the Elcos, and was the immediate forerunner of the 78 ft Higgins boat that would be mass produced for service during the war. In fact PT-70 had been delivered to the Navy some months before the actual competition, time enough for a good deal of testing to be accomplished. The boat drew an enthusiastic response from virtually everyone who had an opportunity to go aboard. The boat handled well, was almost as fast as the Elcos and – of particular delight to the crews – did not pound as hard as the Elcos in a seaway.

One other contender of some note entered the competition, this being the Huckins Yacht Corporation who had built a boat of their own design and at their own expense with a similar agreement as had been made with Higgins – that if the boat proved worthwhile, it would be purchased by the Navy. The craft was powered by four Packard engines (on loan from the Bureau of Ships) situated in two engine rooms.

On each of the days that the tests were conducted very rough sea conditions prevailed producing swells and even waves of the order of fifteen feet. In these conditions the boats performed admirably. During the second race a new destroyer was entered as a control and was given orders to make her best all-out time over the course. During a race that took over six hours to complete, the destroyer Wilkes managed to finish only a few minutes ahead of the leading PT-Boat, one of the Elco 77-footers. The conclusions were obvious. As far as the order of finish was concerned among the PTs, it was determined that the Elco design was the fastest and driest boat, but the Higgins was a very close second with an offsetting advantage of a tighter turning radius than the Elco. The Huckins boat was judged to be overall not as desirable as the Elco or Higgins entries.

The results of the competition were evaluated by the Bureau of Ships and some final specifications for production boats were decided upon. The big three – Sutphen, Higgins and Huckins – were each invited to attend, with their chief engineers, a meeting a few months after the tests, at which time the Navy's requirements would be made known. At the meeting the men were told that the Navy wanted improved designs submitted for approval for boats of between 75 to 82 feet

in length. The Navy felt the increased size was necessary for the amount of ordnance the boats would carry. The companies involved were invited to submit bids for their new boats, and when this was done it turned out that Elco was awarded a contract for thirty-six examples of their new 80 ft design, Higgins was given the nod for the construction of twenty-four of their 78 ft boats and Huckins was contracted to build eight of their craft. All boats would be powered with the now standard Packard engine.

By the time the last of the three contracts was let for the new batch of boats it was December 1941. The outbreak of war with Japan ensured orders beyond the initial agreements. But it would be several months before any of these new boats would be ready for service. In the meantime the Navy would have to make do with the boats it had on hand. These, of course, were the twenty-nine Elco 77-footers which had been delivered during the summer of 1941 and were now dispersed among Squadrons 1, 2 and 3 as described in the first chapter. Perhaps more than any other phrase – judging by what fate had in store for many of these early boats – they were indeed expendable.

Top Right
The Huckins Yacht Corporation of Jacksonville, Florida constructed an experimental PT-Boat at their own expense for competition in the 'Plywood Derbies' of July 1941. The arrangement was that if the boat proved to be satisfactory in performance it would be purchased by the United States Navy. The 72 ft boat was powered by four Packard engines on loan from the Navy, and based on its performance in the derbies a contract was let to Huckins for the construction of eight boats. The design for the production boats was changed considerably, however, to increase the length to 78 feet, with power to be provided by three rather than four engines – all of this at the Navy's request. The 72 ft experimental boat pictured here was purchased by the Navy and given the designation PT-69, but it was never placed in service with a squadron and was finally reclassified as a district patrol vessel (YP-106) in September 1942.

Bottom Right
PTs 3, 4 and 9 were all delivered to the United States Navy during June 1940 at which time Motor Torpedo Boat Squadron 1 was commissioned. Two boats of the three-boat squadron are seen in this photo taken shortly after the commissioning ceremony. Right from the first the Navy established the practice of commissioning a squadron into active duty rather than individual boats, thus saving administrative red tape. Note in this photograph that the plexiglass blisters on PT-9's .50 caliber gun turrets are fogged over on the inside. For this reason the blisters would be removed in favor of open mounts on later Elco boats.

3
The Myth of the United States PT-Boat

'Oh some PT's do seventy knots

And some do sixty-nine

But if we get ours going at all

We think we're doing fine.'

(A popular World War Two PT sailor beer drinking lyric.)

As pointed out earlier, American PT-Boats were born in a cloud of controversy. Advocates felt that their high speed, maneuverability and small size would make them untouchable. Opponents of the concept considered the frailty of the craft and their lack of armor and coined the phrase 'suicide boats'. Realistic experts, both in and out of the navy, agreed on one thing: Even if PTs could press home an attack on a full size warship, the survivability of the small craft would be very much in doubt.

Whether or not they could be of any real use in wartime, the boats made great copy for pre-war newspapers and magazines. They were fast and flashy, their crews cocky and their officers confident – or at least so it seemed. But then the United States was not at war and it would be fair to say that not one American PT-Boat skipper had ever been in combat. Movie-goers of the time got an occasional glimpse of something flashing by a newsreel camera, engulfed in white froth and moving at seemingly phenomenal speed. From the beginning, imaginations began to run a bit wild. Some reports claimed the PTs capable of ranging 3,000 miles on a patrol, incredible as it may sound, when a 400 mile patrol would have been quite ambitious. Much was made of the boats' hitting power, as the underwater torpedo was generally regarded as the single most destructive weapon of modern naval warfare. Unfortunately this ability was much overstated – as was to be learned soon enough. But the greatest PT myth concerned speed. They could achieve a top speed of from 40 to 45 knots under ideal conditions, though war produced conditions that were seldom if ever ideal. It was not uncommon, however, to read magazine accounts of PT-Boats making 70 mph in a fifteen-foot sea.

Some of these exaggerated claims undoubtedly owed their origin to over-

enthuasiastic reporters who, lacking specific and often classified information, frequently used comparative statements to describe performance. The idea of a PT-Boat being able to pace an automobile was often used. Vague comparisons between PT-Boats and aircraft were even printed, with the implication that the former was a match for the latter in terms of all-out speed. What now seems completely unreasonable was then a tangible if somewhat fuzzy concept – as seen through the eyes of the American public – of a craft capable of such performance that it could with ease destroy enemy warships met under any conditions.

Indeed, if a boat were capable of 70 mph speeds in 1940, its chances of surviving an attack on an enemy warship might actually have been favorable under certain conditions. In fact, however, during the early war period in the Pacific most of the PT-Boats were only capable of speeds of between 26 to 35 knots. Fresh replacements for the high-performance engines were, for one reason or another, almost always in short supply. Many engines did double and even triple their recommended life-span of 600

Illustrations such as this appearing in national magazines with accompanying stories about the 'mighty midgets' and the 'little giant killers' contributed significantly to the myth that grew up around PT-Boats. The drawing obviously suggests that a PT is capable of speeds comparative with airplanes.

hours, and tired engines made for slow boats. Yet another factor which cut the PTs' speed was lack of adequate hull maintenance facilities in the forward areas, often resulting in a beard of green marine growth below the waterline or a waterlogged hull long overdue for a drying-out period. At these reduced speeds PT-Boats could be run down easily by fast Japanese destroyers. Thus a PT-Boat's best chance for success was surprise night attack, and its only hope for survival was the confusion of night action which would allow its small silhouette to avoid Japanese searchlights long enough for it to lose itself in the shallow waters of a nearby jungle island.

The myth of the PT-Boat was further strengthened at the outbreak of the war by two more factors. First, the attack on Pearl Harbor left a tremendous gap between the relative numbers of the United States and

Japanese fleets. Americans needed *something* on which to pin their hopes. They needed something in which to place their confidence at a time when humiliation and helplessness were the words of the day. The public was more than willing to take to heart official statements such as that typified by Rear Admiral H.L. Brinser when he termed the PTs '... the best offensive weapon of the Navy'. The PTs unwittingly took on an image they could not possibly hope to fulfill.

The second factor contributing to the PT-Boats' popularity and mythical status was the early action of the small craft in the Philippine Islands as depicted in a popular book entitled *They Were Expendable*. The book, which was an immediate success, romanticized the exploits of Squadron 3 and made particular note of General Douglas MacArthur's exciting escape from the Islands via the speedy little craft. Newspaper stories – and even comic strips of the time – elaborated further on these early exploits to the extent that one wondered whether the PTs were not capable of winning the war in the Pacific singlehanded. As we shall soon

see, what actually happened in the Philippines during those early days of the war takes on a considerably different tone when examined from an objective historical standpoint.

EARLY ACTION IN THE PHILIPPINES

'The Americans have a new weapon – a monster that roars, flaps its wings, and fires torpedoes in all directions.'
From a captured Japanese war diary.

Many of the questions concerning the effectiveness of the PT-Boat were seemingly answered by the exploits of Squadron 3 in the Philippines where it operated from the beginning of the war until April 1942. In the first air attacks on the Manila area almost all the PTs' spare parts, machine shop, gasoline, and torpedoes were lost. PT-Boats were unlike larger ships in that they could not remain self-sufficient for long periods of time. The PTs, like aircraft, required constant maintenance. Although they were forced to operate under these adverse con-

An extremely rare photograph taken before the beginning of the war showing three of Squadron 3's 77-footers idling into the harbor at Manila. The understrength squadron had only six boats at the time hostilities began, including PTs 31 through 35 and 41.

ditions, the boats of Squadron 3 proved invaluable in General MacArthur's defense of the Islands, and they were involved in many gunnery actions with barges and shore installations while on nightly patrols. While it was generally held that PT-Boats were supposed to be the opponents of capital ships, the men of Squadron 3 could have had little idea that this business of night gunnery action in connection with Japanese activity around the thousands of islands in the South Pacific would come to be the major role of the PT-Boats throughout the Pacific War.

But the PTs fired torpedoes in the Philippines as well. They claimed four sinkings in the five months they operated, the climax being a large Japanese cruiser on the night of 8 April. By that time only two of the six boats originally assigned to the squadron were operable and afloat.

PT-41 under Squadron Commander Lt John D. Bulkeley and PT-34 skippered by Lt Robert B. Kelly (portrayed loosely by John Wayne in the 1946 movie version of *They Were Expendable*) were on patrol off Cebu on the evening of 8 April when they spotted what they believed to be a six-inch gunned cruiser either of the *Tenryu* or *Kuma* class rounding a point of the island. The boats crept to within 500 yards of the unsuspecting cruiser and attacked. Eight torpedoes were fired that night and unfortunately the old Mark VIIIs were up to their old tricks of running off course or failing to explode when striking a target from a 90° angle. The first two torpedoes fired by the 41 boat ran erratically. Bulkeley, having completed a tight circle, then fired his second two 'fish', which were seen to run straight and true only to fail to explode after hitting the cruiser amidships. Two duds! The cruiser suddenly came to life. Searchlights flashed on and gun crews began firing at the attackers. Kelly pressed his attack home while Bulkeley attempted to draw fire, passing close along the port side of the Japanese warship, pouring machine-gun fire into her decks. After Kelly's first two torpedoes missed astern he circled around behind the ship to come up from almost dead astern. The 34 boat fired her last two torpedoes in an overtaking shot, then turned to retire. The cruiser turned with

the PT, apparently in an attempt to block escape. As the big ship swung hard to port two spouts of water amidships were observed through binoculars by Kelly. One of two things had happened. Either the cruiser had turned directly into the last two torpedoes and they had exploded, or she had been struck accidently by shellfire from an escorting destroyer that was following behind the cruiser and had opened up on the PTs. The former seems the most likely explanation. The cruiser's searchlights immediately faded as though there had been a power failure. Bulkeley noted that the cruiser was soon enveloped in a cloud of yellowish brown smoke and that as a destroyer swept by and briefly illuminated the stricken ship, 'It could be seen that the cruiser was sinking by the stern with her bow up in the air.' Although the Japanese reported no ship losses that night, the action was witnessed from the shore by at least two individuals, an Army private and an American professor from the local university: both were sure that the cruiser had gone down.

This battle set a pattern that would haunt PT actions for the rest of the war. Whether a ship was struck and sunk that night remains in doubt to this day; there is conflicting evidence on both sides of the argument. But at the time the American public enthusiastically accepted the claims of the PT sailors.

PT-32, one of the 'expendables' of the Philippines campaign had a short but very active life during the opening months of World War Two. The 77-footer is seen here on her trials off the East Coast during July 1941. While in the Philippines PT-32 earned the distinction of carrying more people aboard than any other PT of the war. On the night of 17 December the 32 along with PTs 34 and 35 went to the rescue of the SS *Corregidor* which had hit a mine while leaving Manila en route for Australia. The ship was loaded with evacuees. Throughout the night the PT crews picked up survivors, and when the boats finally reached *Corregidor* the following morning and made a head count it was found that PT-32 had picked up 196 passengers. Later in the campaign the 32 attacked what was believed to be a Japanese cruiser off the Bataan shore on the night of 1 February. Closing to within 5,000 yards PT-32 launched two torpedoes, one of which apparently struck the cruiser amidships, although this could never be confirmed. PT-32 was finally destroyed by friendly fire after completing her last mission of evacuating a portion of General MacArthur's Party. At the time she was a floating wreck, with only one engine in operation. She was, indeed, expendable.

4
Production and Modification

'With daring and fearless young Naval officers like
Lieutenant Bulkeley and Lieutenant Kelly, there is nothing
but trouble and defeat ahead for the enemy. The Navy is
anxious to use these men. To do that it must have more of
these boats. We need them now. Tomorrow may be too late.'

(Rear Admiral Adolphus Andrews addressing Elco factory workers on the occasion of the
launching of PT-103, the first 80-footer, on 16 May 1942.)

BOAT CONSTRUCTION

When we last left the home front at the end of
the second chapter, the Navy had just
awarded contracts to three manufacturers for
a substantial production run of new boats.
Higgins and Huckens were awarded their
contracts in the fall of 1941, while the new
Elco contract was not formally released until
December. But by that time world events had
taken rather a dramatic turn, and there was
little question that Elco would in the future
be able to sell all the PT-Boats they could
build.

By the beginning of World War Two Elco
had delivered twenty-nine examples of their
77 ft boat to the Navy. While plans were
being made to shift production over to the
new 80 ft design, Elco still had twenty of the
77-footers to construct and deliver on the
earlier contract. These remaining twenty
boats were all delivered by mid-March 1942,
but in the meantime the phased cutover to the
80 ft design had begun with the keel laying of
PT-103 during late January. This first of the
new boats was not completed until 16 May,
when it was lowered by crane into the water at
the Bayonne plant amid considerable cere-

mony. High-ranking company officials,
Navy admirals and politicians all made
speeches to the assembled factory workers
and news media. The highlight of the morning was an address by Lt John D. Bulkeley,
recently returned from his exploits as Squadron Commander of the now defunct Squadron 3 in the Philippines. Much to the delight
of the crowd, he described some of his

Shortly after its launching, the first Elco 80-footer
– PT-103 – was photographed during one of many
trial runs. This was the profile that the American
public would come to associate with the words
'PT-Boat'.

adventures, fulsomely praising the workman-ship and durability of his squadron's 77-Elcos, and then urged the workers on to greater production efforts. The sleek new 80 ft boat was carefully set into the water and then, again much to the delight and surprise of many of the onlookers, her engines were fired up and she roared off into the bay. PT-103 marked the beginning of a production run that would span three years almost to the day when the last of the Elco 80-footers, PT-760, would be delivered to the Navy in a knocked-down form for shipment to Russia as a lend-lease product. During that time the basic design of the boat would remain virtually unchanged.

While the new design was only three feet longer than the 77-footers, it was an entirely different boat that capitalized on Elco's previous experience and thoroughly over-came the weaknesses of the earlier boats. Weighing in at 38 tons, compared to the 77-footers' displacement of 33 tons, the 80-footer was slightly slower than the 77-footers and not quite as maneuverable. It was, however, a better riding boat, particularly in a seaway, and could carry a greater warload than the earlier boats.

The construction process for the 80 ft Elco was much the same as for the 77-footers and was rather innovative for its time. First, the main supporting structure of the boats – the main frames or bulkheads – were pre-fabricated. They were constructed of lam-inated spruce, white oak and mahogany with all joints being secured with screws and marine glue. These skeletal structures were then covered on both sides with marine plywood and sealed for water-tight integrity. The completed bulkheads were then placed upside-down in jigs arranged on the floor of

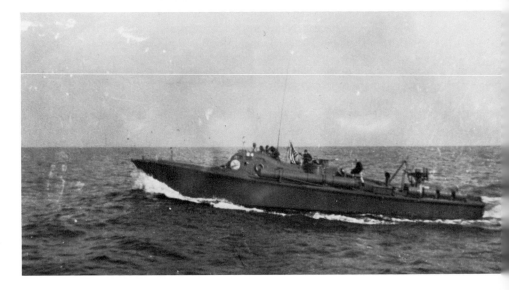

Top
One of the great PT-Boat action photos of all time. Two Mark VIII torpedoes leap from the forward tubes of an Elco 80-footer during test firing exercises off Rhode Island in 1943.

Center
An officer aboard PT-64 clowns for the camera while his boat is tied up at Moorehead City on a training cruise during early 1942. This view provides a good look at the cockpit arrangement aboard the late series Elco 77-footers, these boats having the sloped cabin roof and manually operated machine-gun turrets minus the plexiglass domes.

Bottom
PT-64 cruises off Cape Hatteras on an anti-submarine training patrol during early 1942. This Squadron 4 boat – part of the Melville training group – carries only the two forward torpedo tubes, depth charges replacing the two aft. It was thought that the boats might serve a sub-chaser function, an idea which happened to coincide with production problems for the 21 in. torpedo tubes so that not all boats could be equipped with four tubes anyway.

38

the main assembly area. The next step was to tie all the bulkheads together with the keel, which was secured with brass bolts. Next came the chines, the joining point for the bottom and sides of the boat. With these three items in place, additional longitudinal and diagonal battens were attached to the hull in preparation for the planking. The planking was then applied in two layers running diagonally to each other and consisting of mahogany boards six inches wide and one inch thick. The planking was fastened to the main frames with screws and to the battens with copper nails. Between the two layers of planking was sandwiched sheets of aircraft fabric soaked in marine glue, this adding substantially to the strength and water-tight integrity of the hull.

With the hull planking completed, the now fully formed hull was turned over in place to receive a similarly planked deck. Next came the superstructure items consisting of little more than spruce framers covered on both sides with plywood. While in the upright

position on the main floor, the remaining hardware items, including fuel tanks, engines and running gear, were also added and the interior finished off. While it is true that some plywood was used in the construction of the boats, it is clear to see from the above that such descriptive terms as 'Plywood Wonders' and 'Plywood Derby' were really inaccurate in that the PTs were built largely of other materials. The production methods introduced by Elco were so efficient that virtually every boat they produced throughout the war was delivered ahead of schedule.

Other than the two Elco designs, the only other PT-Boats to see combat in the service of the United States Navy during World War Two were the 78-footers built by Higgins. The eight boats completed by Huckins on their first and only contract were found to be inferior to the other designs, displaying in particular some rather poor handling characteristics. They were, throughout the war, relegated to training duties off the East Coast and in Hawaiian waters.

Two PT-Boat crewmembers pose for a prewar photograph aboard their Elco 77 ft boat. The Walt Disney-designed insignia of a mosquito carrying a torpedo stemmed from the often-used nickname 'mosquito boats'. Although the crewmen are unidentified, the photograph was probably taken at the New York Navy Yard just before the United States entered the war.

This sequence of photographs shows the progressive steps in hull construction at the Elco plant. The boat is an 80 ft model which begins life upside-down. After the hull planking is applied, the craft is turned right side up and construction begins on the deck. Note the dayroom assembly in the foreground sitting across the bow of another 80 ft boat.

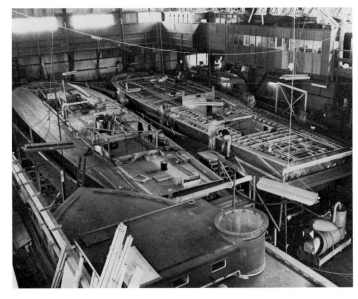

The Navy Department expressed its appreciation to Elco in mid-1942 with this letter. Innovative construction techniques, solid designs and patriotic factory workers were all integral parts of the Elco effort.

DEPARTMENT OF THE NAVY
OFFICE OF THE UNDER SECRETARY
WASHINGTON

July 22, 1942

Mr. Henry R. Sutphen, Vice-President
Electric Boat Company
Elco Naval Division
33 Pine Street
New York, New York

Dear Mr. Sutphen:

This is to inform you that the Army and Navy are conferring upon the Elco Naval Division the Army-Navy Production Award for high achievement in the production of war equipment.

This award consists of a flag to be flown above the honored plant, and a lapel pin, significant of major contribution to victory, for every member of this Division.

The high and practical patriotism of the men and women of the Elco Naval Division of the Electric Boat Company is inspiring and heartening. Their record will be difficult to surpass, yet the Army and Navy have every confidence that it was made only to be broken.

Sincerely yours,

James Forrestal

Bottom
Elco 77 ft PT-Boats proceed in column during exercises off New York during late 1941. Note the twin-engine Army scout bomber just to the left of the first boat. To the left of the flag in the foreground can be seen part of the early smoke-generating device. The high freeboard and relatively flat bottom of the early Elco boats – very evident in this photograph – made them the fastest operational American PT-Boats, but also the most uncomfortable since they tended to pound heavily in a seaway.

As far as Andrew Higgins is concerned, his company managed to turn out 199 of his 78 foot boats, of which 146 saw service with the United States Navy while the remainder were shipped to England and Russia. As pointed out earlier, the Higgins design had characteristics all its own. Stubbier in appearance than the graceful Elco designs, Higgins boats were often referred to as a box with a point on one end, a reference obviously invoked by Elco crew-members to provoke the ire of Higgins devotees. With fresh engines, the Higgins 78 ft design could make 41 knots, a knot or so slower than the Elco 80-footers. But the Higgins boats could turn circles around the later Elcos, and although their crews paid the price of being drenched by such maneuvers, such a capability was an important asset for close-in fighting with barges and avoiding attacking aircraft. Clearly the Higgins approach was more of a utilitarian design than the Elcos, based on the Higgins reputation for building stout and very rugged workboats.

With its cockpit located between the two twin .50 caliber machine-gun turrets and just aft of a small charthouse, the machine-gunners had a more limited field of fire than their counterparts on the Elco 80-footers. Like the early Elco boats, the Higgins PTs carried four heavy steel torpedo tubes on the generally unobstructed after portion of the deck. But where the Elco tubes were normally stowed inboard and had to be cranked out into firing position when action was imminent, the tubes aboard the Higgins boats were fixed permanently in place and angled out at 12 degrees from the centerline of the boat. Below decks the crews accommodations were small and cramped in contrast to the rather roomy berthing areas found on the Elco 80-footers. On the other hand, nearly half the length of the Higgins design was taken up by a large engine room, while the Elco boats had rather small, but certainly well arranged, engineering areas. The long engine room aboard the Higgins boats allowed all three of the engines to drive their propeller shafts directly, whereas the Elco boats used a V-drive system to transmit power from the two wing engines while the center engine alone drove its shaft directly. The V-drives were only a disadvantage in that the extra gearing tended to cut down very slightly on engine output, and the units were just one more piece of equipment that had to be maintained and could fail at a critical time. It should be noted that late in the war Elco completely redesigned the engine room on the 80-footers so as to allow the three engines to drive directly and eliminate the need for V-drives.

The first squadron of Higgins boats was not commissioned until September of 1942, the first few boats having been completed the month before. True to the luck of its number, Squadron 13 had problems from the first. These first boats taken over by squadron officers in New Orleans were found to be overweight and not up to performance in the matter of top speed. Squadron officers and officers of the commissioning detail based in New Orleans went to work on the problem with the builder. Soon they had lightened the boats substantially and made other internal and external modifications in equipment that considerably increased the handling and performance of the boats. The changes were then incorporated in all future Higgins production.

But Squadron 13's luck was not about to change, for they were soon given the unpleasant task of being shipped to the Aleutian Islands where the worst enemy to be encountered would be the miserable living and operating conditions. The next squadron-sized batch of boats produced by Higgins was delivered to the Russians on lend-lease. Finally, five months after the commissioning of the first Higgins boat squadron, a second squadron was commissioned in January 1943. Squadron 15 would be the first to take the 78 ft Higgins boat into combat, beginning with deployment to the Mediterranean in April 1943. The numerous and rather wild exploits of this squadron are detailed in a following chapter.

ENGINES

The work done between the wars by the Packard engine company in conjunction with the racing efforts and financial support of Gar Wood (whose accomplishments have been outlined already) made possible the availability of an excellent source of power for all the operational PT-Boats produced during World War Two. The 12-cylinder Packard Marine Engine 4M-2500 – an outgrowth of the famous 750 hp Liberty aircraft engine introduced in 1925 by Packard's Colonel J.G. Vincent – was a highly dependable light-weight unit producing 1,200 hp in its early production version. Later in the war the engine's output was increased to 1,350 hp and then finally to 1,500 hp. Although the potential for significant increases in speed was there with these later engines, the power increases coincided with the ever increasing warloads carried by the boats so that, generally, performance remained the same as with the early boats. Typically, the 1,350 hp version, with its gear-driven centrifugal supercharger, produced its maximum rated power output at 2,400 rpm and 41.2 inches of mercury manifold pressure. Three engines running at this speed in an 80 foot Elco boat

An excellent rear view of PT-63 tied up at Moorehead City during early 1942. After a year with the training squadron at Melville this boat would be transferred to Squadron 5 for shipment to the Solomons, where it would see considerable action until destroyed by a fire in port during June 1944.

would consume almost 500 gallons of 100 octane aviation gasoline in one hour. At a cruising speed of 35 knots produced with the maximum sustained rpm rating for the engines of 2,000 rpm, the same boat would consume about 300 gallons of gasoline giving the boat a range of 520 miles with a typical full fuel load of 3,000 gallons.

It was soon learned that if PT-Boats were going to do anybody any good they would have to be based near the front lines of fighting. This meant operating from advanced bases – mostly of a temporary nature as the battle areas generally changed with some frequency. Those boats that were heavily involved in combat operations virtually always were a step ahead of full or even adequate maintenance centers. This had a particularly telling effect on the engines, which were often called upon to do double their recommended duty of 600 hours before overhaul. But the Packards stood up admirably and earned a well-deserved reputation for reliability considering their high-performance nature. On a number of

occasions engines received severe battle damage or were called upon to operate while partially submerged due to damage to the hull. But again, like any high-performance engine, they were also known to fail at very inopportune times. Luckily such instances were rare. It is interesting to note that within the confines of an 80 ft boat, often displacing over 50 tons loaded weight, the power produced by these engines was such that a noticeable torque condition had to be allowed for, particularly at low rpm. At mid-range speeds the torque was not a factor but as top speed was reached, torque from the three propellers all turning in the same direction would tend to throw the stern to port as much as 3° and rudder compensation was again necessary. While many of the exaggerated pre-war claims made for the PT-Boats' performance certainly are not true, with the power of the three Packards a PT-Boat was, indeed, an outstanding performer. In waves up to 4-feet high, a PT could proceed on any course at full speed. Through as high as an 8-foot sea a boat could withstand full speed

This photograph clearly shows the cockpit arrangement of an Elco 80-footer. This PT is one of the earlier series 80-footers, identifiable through the arrangement of the boat controls. A common and favored practice was for two men to control the boat during operation, one man at the helm and one at the throttles. On later series boats, to facilitate this arrangement, the throttle controls were moved over to the right-hand-side of the wheel providing adequate space for two men to stand side by side. Note that the light armor shield normally installed at the rear of the cockpit has been removed in the field. Many boat skippers felt it was unfair for them to be protected by any sort of steel armor while the rest of the crew had only plywood for protection (which was as good as nothing at all), and the armor plate was thus often removed.

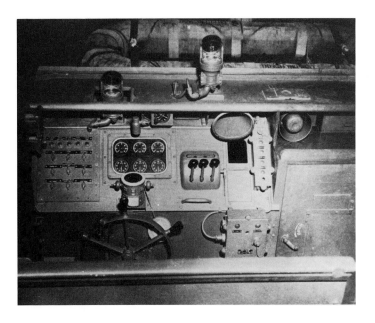

Top Left
A view of the instrumentation on a later-series Elco boat. Note that the throttle controls have been moved over to the right side of the wheel to facilitate two-man operation of the boat. Immediately in front of the wheel is one of the boat's three compasses and an instrument panel. The three top gauges indicate individual engine rpm while the three lower gauges show engine oil pressure. To the left of the wheel is the weapons control panel including torpedo firing switches.

Top Right
An Elco 80-footer cuts across the wake of another boat causing the PT's bow to come high out of the water. Lack of radar identifies this boat as one of the early numbered craft.

Center Right
This was the view from the cockpit of an Elco 80-footer. A wooden motor boat with a 20 ft beam seems quite impressive in size when viewed from this perspective. Guard rail for the forward .50 caliber turret is on the right. This photograph also illustrates one other point. Note the foamy white wake produced by the two boats ahead. It was this trail that was so easy for enemy aircraft to follow or for Japanese destroyer lookouts to spot – even at night thanks to phosphorous glow. Although a number of experiments were carried out throughout the war to try to reduce the wake, none were successful.

Bottom Right
A closeup view of the port side superstructure of an Elco 80 ft boat, PT-107, one of the first boats of the 80 ft type produced (the series beginning with PT-103). Note that the boat is equipped with the early type mast: radar not yet being available for the boats. After having reached the South Pacific with Squadron 5 during the spring of 1943 this boat participated in combat operations for almost one year before being destroyed by a gas dock fire along with PT-63 while fueling at the island of Emirau.

Top Left
Three Elco boats of Squadron 7 running in formation off the Panama Canal during late 1942. In addition to performing the necessary patrol duties, duty in Panama allowed the squadron valuable training time before going into combat in the Solomons in July 1943.

Top Right
An Elco 77 ft boat is seen in this wartime view taken at the Melville training center. Of the forty-nine examples of the 77-footer built by Elco, beginning with PT-44 the factory made a few small superstructure changes including the addition of a radio direction finder on the top starboard side of the chartroom.

Center Right
Squadron 4, the training squadron based at Melville, Rhode Island, was commissioned during January 1942, and received during that same month several brand-new Elco 77-footers including the two boats pictured here. As can be seen, however, the winter months of 1942 were something less than pleasant in the way of weather conditions. As this photo was taken sister boats in the Philippines were fighting the advancing Japanese. PTs 60 through 68 were originally configured from the factory with only two tubes each, the aft spaces being used to carry depth charges in the vain hope that the boats could be used as anti-submarine craft. PTs 60 and 61 were among those boats later sent to the Solomons to do battle with the 'Tokyo Express', and on several occasions their lack of two additional torpedoes was sorely felt. PTs 62 through 68 remained with the training squadron well into 1943. Although the boat in the foreground of this photo is unidentified, the boat on the other side of the dock is PT-65.

Bottom Right
Broadside view of the aft section of a Melville training squadron 77-footer. The starboard turret gunner is practising live firing. The depth charges and 20 mm cannon normally mounted on the aft deck were apparently taken ashore for this exercise.

operation with a little judicious helmsmanship to keep the boat from landing too hard against a swell with the possible result of a cracked deck or frame member. But such performance certainly reduced the life expectancy of hull and engines not to mention the fact that a crew generally had less endurance than their boat. As far as boats in combat theaters were concerned, knowing that their lives might depend on the reliability of their boats, PTs were usually treated roughly only when absolutely necessary.

ARMAMENT

As a general statement, one can say that as the war progressed, the armament carried aboard PT-Boats increased to the point where they could honestly be called, pound-for-pound, the most heavily armed craft within the entire United States Navy. All boats left the factories with a standard armament package that was modified on a production basis from time to time to take advantage of new technology as well as field demands. It will also be noted, however, that many boats were heavily and progressively modified once they reached the combat areas. This activity was certainly facilitated to a considerable extent by the relative ease of making rearrangements and additions to a small wooden boat. Modifications were not so prevalent during the early combat tours such as in the Guadalcanal campaign, but once the PTs began to be used as gunboats and barge-busters, the modification tempo increased.

Nominal armament for the first boats to see combat for the United States – the original twenty-nine Elco 77-footers, included four Mark VIII torpedoes carried in heavy welded steel tubes, four .50 caliber Browning machine-guns set in twin mounts situated on the port and starboard side a few feet aft of the cockpit, a single 20 mm Oerlikon M-4 gun atop a Mark 4 hand elevated mount and two .30 caliber Lewis machine-guns, one mounted on a small swivel on the bow and one set on the starboard side of the cockpit. The Lewis guns were normally carried stowed below deck, and were only brought out when combat was imminent. Primarily intended as a light anti-aircraft weapon, they were virtually ineffectual and were soon abandoned in favor of heavier automatic weapons. In addition to the above, each boat carried a complete selection of small arms including .45 caliber pistols, rifles, submachine-guns and even an occasional hand grenade – which came to be used primarily by the cook for fishing, at least in the forward areas.

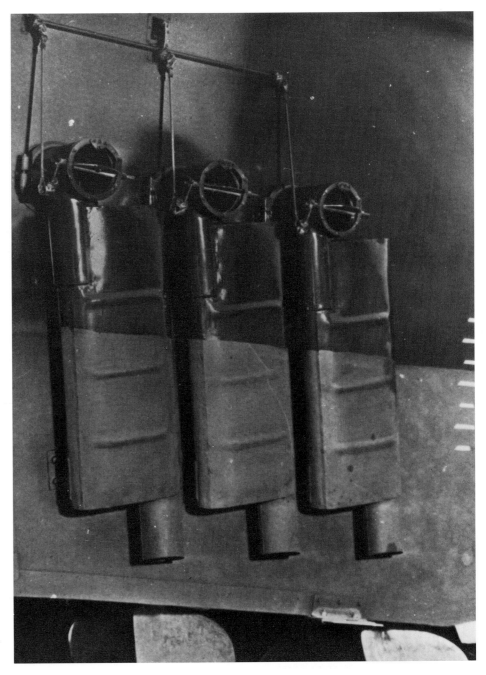

The torpedoes carried by American PT-Boats were a disgrace. As pointed out earlier, they were of World War One vintage. Designed to be fired from destroyers, they were heavy and slow and carried a relatively small warhead which was eventually proven to be activated by an often defective firing mechanism. In tests it was found that some 63 per cent of all Mark VIII torpedoes were defective and would not detonate as a result of a direct hit, but rather had to hit a target from an angle before exploding. What is more, with the early Elco 77 ft and 80 ft boats, the torpedoes were fired from their tubes via a black powder charge. The torpedoes were heavily greased and oiled before insertion

A closeup of the port side of the transom of an Elco 80-footer reveals the details of the muffler installation. A single actuating rod running into the engine room passes through the stern and connects to three smaller rods which in turn are connected to butterfly valves in the exhaust pipes. When the butterfly valves are open, the engines are running with their exhausts virtually unrestricted. With the valves in the closed position, the exhaust gasses are routed down through the mufflers and exit, depending on the speed of the boat, into the water. With the muffler system engaged, care had to be taken not to run the engines at too high an rpm to prevent intolerable levels of backpressure. Engines were always started with the valves in the open position.

into the tubes to ensure a smooth ejection, but the black powder often ignited the oil in the tube as the torpedo left, causing a brilliant red flash. This happened on several occasions during combat operations, particularly in the early Solomons campaign against the 'Tokyo Express'. This naturally gave the boat's position away to the enemy, spoiling a typically unobserved attack and providing an excellent target. In addition, while the torpedo theoretically left the tube at a velocity of 40 feet per second, clearing the deck by some five and a half feet, partial misfires occasionally caused the torpedo to bang its vanes against the deck on the way out resulting in an erratic run. Worse, torpedoes occasionally failed to leave the tubes, the warhead hanging out over the side of the boat with the torpedo motor on a 'hot run'. In such a situation a scant few seconds were available before the motor disintegrated. Although there was no danger of the warhead going off, the explosion of the motor would send lethal fragments of shrapnel zinging through the tube and over the deck. As pointed out earlier, Higgins boats had their tubes installed in a fixed position while all of the Elco boats made use of a turntable rear

Top Right
Scott-Paine of British Power Boat worked for years to convince the British Admiralty that they should obtain a force of motor torpedo boats. But when the Admiralty finally decided to go full speed ahead with the concept they bought the vast majority of their boats from Vosper, beginning with this 70 ft version. Powered by the American Packard engine, they were good boats but were too small for United States needs, although many were built in American yards and delivered to Great Britain. Disappointed but not defeated, Scott-Paine took his excellent 70 ft design and sold it elsewhere – namely to the United States Navy.

Center Right
PT-103, the first of the new breed of Elco boats, passes up the 'Slot' on the way to its new operating base at Rendova, refueling en route from an escorting tender. As a member of Squadron 5 the boat had spent nearly a year patrolling off Panama – guarding the Canal – before being reassigned to the Solomons in July 1943.

Bottom Right
PTs 71 and 72 were the first two production Higgins 78-footers and were based on the 76 ft PT-70 which competed in the Plywood Derbies. PT-72 spent the first two years of its life at the Melville, Long Island PT-Boat training facility as an element of Squadron 4. During March 1944, at the urgent request of the British, this boat – along with PTs 71 and 199 – took its place in the smallest PT squadron ever commissioned for operational use. The new unit was designated Squadron 2, that number being vacant after the dissolution of the original Squadron 2 in the Solomons during November 1943. The three boats were sent to England where – equipped with special navigational equipment – they operated on special, often clandestine, missions across the English Channel. This photograph shows the 72 during its Squadron 4 days at Melville.

support and a hand-operated steel lead-screw traveling within a swiveling cut made fast to the tube forward support. When action was imminent, the forward tubes were hand-cranked out to their stop position of $8\frac{1}{2}°$ overboard, and the rear tubes to $12\frac{1}{2}°$ overboard.

Once the torpedoes were fired, preset gyro angles brought the weapons back on to their desired course. As far as aiming the torpedoes was concerned, it was basically a matter of aiming the boat in the direction of a collision course with the moving target. Each boat came equipped with a torpedo director mounted on the bridge. The torpedo track arm was set parallel to the centerline of the boat while the target track arm could be swung about to sight the intended victim. The only problem with this device – as well as with the Mark 7 portable angle solver consisting of a series of plastic discs and a celluloid runner and commonly referred to as an 'izwas' machine – was that one had to be able to see and track the target. During the Solomons campaign, for instance, virtually all the intercepts were made in the black of night when ranges were so short by the time a target was spotted that there was little opportunity or need to use a director. One simply pointed one's boat at the enemy and let fly.

The black powder charges which launched the torpedoes were set off electrically by firing switches on the bridge. This gave the skipper of a boat the best possible control. However, in the event of a malfunction during action, a torpedoman crouched by each tube with a wooden mallet in hand to hit a manual percussion cap. Standard practice was to retard the throttles at the moment of launch to allow the torpedoes to clear the tubes, and it was most desirable to have the boat on a steady keel, tubes as horizontal as possible at the instant of firing. Any combination from one to all four tubes could be fired at one time, although the most favored practice seemed to be to fire the two aft tubes and then the two forward tubes at the same time. The reason for this was because after firing two torpedoes a boat might cruise for hours before launching its last two fish. Very simply, a PT with its after two tubes empty was in better trim and could make more speed than with its forward tubes empty.

The advisability of finding a new torpedo launching system – and indeed a new torpedo – was understood by everyone who had anything to do with PT-Boats. Late in 1942 experiments were conducted at the now sprawling motor torpedo boat training center at Melville, Rhode Island that involved a boat davit-like arrangement whereby the torpedoes could be swung out over the side of the boat and simply dropped into the water.

Unfortunately, the system was judged not sturdy enough for use aboard bucking 80 ft speedboats. Legend has it that the true innovation in PT weaponry was the result of a bar-room discussion between Lt George Sprugel, Jr and Lt James Costigan on an evening in late February 1943. The two officers of PT-188 reasoned that a simple roll-off device could be constructed to allow one of the newer Mark XIII aircraft torpedoes to slip over the side of a PT-Boat. Such a plan would not have worked with the Mark VIII as its gyro was too sensitive to allow rolling of the torpedo, but the men thought it was worth a try with the Mark XIII.

Based on a few crude sketches, a simple two-piece rack, very similar to those used to hold and roll depth charges over the side of a PT, was constructed at the Scrap Metal Section of the New York Navy Yard. A manually operated handle attached to a series of cables and pulleys started the gyro and motor and a moment later let the torpedo slide down the greased skids. The new rack was soon installed aboard PT-188 and, with a borrowed Mark XIII torpedo with exercise

PT-84, one of the first 78 ft Higgins boats, is seen here running in the Gulf of Mexico shortly after her delivery to the Navy in December 1942. Within four months the boat would be operating in the Aleutians as part of Squadron 13.

warhead, tests were conducted at the Navy's torpedo test firing range in Narragansett Bay. Over a period of several days the torpedo was launched, serviced, reloaded and launched again with complete success. It so happened that a captain from the Bureau of Ordnance in Washington was on hand for the tests, and by the time the PT returned to the New York Navy Yard orders had been received to install the new rack on all Squadron 12 boats. This was the beginning of a modification program that would see virtually all PT-Boats in service, as well as those constructed in the future, equipped with the new racks and armed with Mark XIII torpedoes. Unfortunately for the PT-Boats, by the time most of the squadrons were equipped with the Mark XIII the really juicy targets such as those encountered in the Solomons were nowhere to be found. Many boats had two and later even all of their torpedoes removed when they went out on barge-busting patrols, this allowing them to carry more automatic weapons on deck. At that point they simply became fast gunboats.

The two twin .50 caliber machine-gun mounts carried by all PT-Boats was a versatile and hard-hitting weapons system.

Good for anti-personnel, anti-ship and anti-aircraft work, they remained standard armament on all boats throughout the war. There are reports that some boats operating in the Solomons had their .50 caliber guns removed and 20 mm cannons mounted in the tubs instead, but this seems questionable as it would have been a cumbersome installation and would have required a loader to be perched in a rather precarious position. On the early 77 ft boats – those on hand for the attack on Pearl Harbor as well as the boats that saw action in the Philippines – the twin .50 caliber guns were installed in hydraulically operated, power-driven turrets covered over with a plexiglass blister. The very first actions proved this system to be unsatisfactory, as the hydraulic system could not be used without power and the plexiglass blister often became covered with water spray obscuring the gunner's vision. Thereafter, all PTs were constructed with manually traversed, open machine-gun mounts.

The 20 mm Oerlikon cannon carried on the afterdeck of the early PTs gave the boats considerable hitting power. The high-angle gun had a rate of fire of 450 rounds per

Seen here is the assembly line at the Higgins Industries City Park Plant in New Orleans, showing the advancing stages of construction on a group of 78 ft boats. This photograph would have been taken around January 1943. Barely visible over the large door at the rear of the building is a sign reading 'THE GUY WHO RELAXES IS HELPING THE AXIS'. Higgins production during 1943 – a closely guarded secret at the time – was of the order of seven boats per month.

minute, a range of 5,500 yards and a ceiling of 6,000 feet. Explosive and tracer shells were carried in a sixty-round magazine, the shells being pushed out by a hand-wound watch spring. With its .50 caliber and 20 mm armament, a PT caught in the open by an enemy aircraft had a reasonably good chance of defending itself. But this automatic weapons armament was not nearly heavy enough to deal with the Japanese barges and German Flak Lighters encountered in ever increasing numbers starting in 1943. To this end all manner of field experiments were tried, at least one involving the installation of a 37 mm single-shot cannon, lashed to coconut logs and mounted on the forecastle of a New Guinea-based boat. The slow rate of fire called for a better idea, and this eventually came when someone scavenged an automatic

Top Left

A quarter-stern view of a mid-war 78 ft Higgins boat, PT-462. The boat carries twin 20 mm cannons and launching racks for four Mark XIII torpedoes. The radar mast with its dome on top was designed to fold backward to a stowed position. PT-462 was commissioned as part of the all-Higgins Squadron 31 on 5 April 1944 under the command of none other than the veteran Solomons campaign skipper Jack Searles. This photo was taken a few days after the commissioning. The boat later saw action at Treasury Island in the Solomons during late 1944 and at Palau in the Marianas during the first few months of 1945.

Bottom Left

PT-644 is seen here being lowered into the water at the Higgins plant. When internal or superstructure modifications were designed into production boats, the first boat in the production run that incorporated those changes bore the name of a new 'class'. PT-644 was a member of the PT-625 class, the last and most updated class of Higgins 78-footers produced during the war. While the photograph is dated 1 March 1945, this boat was not officially handed over to the government until May 1945. Three months later PT-644 was among a batch of thirty-two such boats handed over to the Russians on lend-lease.

Top Right

Overhead view of a Higgins boat underway during October 1943. PT-285 was a member of Squadron 23. At the time this photograph was taken the squadron was on its way from New Orleans, where it had been commissioned, to the west coast – by way of the Panama Canal. The boat is seen here on the run up the Central American coast after having passed through the Canal. The squadron would soon be on its way to the South Pacific for barge-busting duty at Bougainville Island.

Bottom Right

A broadside view of a 625-class Higgins boat, PT-631, representing the final word in Higgins production. In addition to the most modern radar, the boat carries a 37 mm gun on the bow flanked by twin 5 in. rocket launchers. The twin caliber machine-guns remained in place throughout the war. Further aft is a single 20 mm gun on a tripod base followed by a 40 mm on the fantail. The boat is equipped with four launching racks for Mark XIII torpedoes. This photograph, taken in March 1945, shows the 631 shortly before being handed over to the Russians along with the rest of the brand new boats of Squadron 43.

37 mm cannon from the nose of a wrecked P-39 Army fighter and, with a few judicious modifications, mounted the gun on a 20 mm pedestal on the bow of an Elco 80-footer. The installation proved to be highly successful, wholesale field modifications being carried out on existing boats with an even more improved arrangement installed on boats delivered by the factory towards the end of the war. With its rate of fire of 120 rounds per minute and range of 8,875 yards, the hard-hitting 37 mm delivered on the later boats had its own special mount set on the centerline of the forward deck, thus replacing the lighter 20 mm pedestal mount.

Early PT-Boat actions were mostly defensive in nature, that is, an attempt to deny the enemy access to a particular area. As such their operating radius was usually short and the actions involved mainly the firing of torpedoes. But as the boats began to move forward in the leap-frogging war in the Pacific, they were literally forced to justify their existence. The Japanese came to rely heavily on inter-island barge traffic as a means for communication and resupply, and as this traffic developed, PT-Boats were the only effective weapon on hand to combat it. Hugging the coastlines of jungle islands and traveling only at night, barges were difficult to detect with aircraft and were too close to shore to be dealt with by heavier surface ships. Traditional gunboats might have been effective, but a traditional gunboat was a relatively slow craft, unable to reach patrol areas as far away as 200 miles from their base by nightfall and return the next day. Furthermore, in the Pacific such gunboats were not available in any numbers – but PT-Boats were. With this task in mind, the 40 mm Bofors gun was soon being field-installed on boats in the Pacific, this requiring the relocation of the 20 mm cannon up on the bow with the 37 mm. This was a typical arrangement, although some boats actually mounted their 40 mm on the bow. This, however, placed a tremendous strain on the forward deck and tended to work loose and crack bulkheads and planking. The 40 mm cannon was the real answer to barge-busting. With a rate of fire of 130 rounds per minute and a range of 5,420 yards, the explosive shells from this hard-hitting weapon could punch holes in virtually any Japanese small craft the PTs of 1944 and 1945 were likely to encounter. One of the major reasons the Bofors gun could be carried was the elimination of the heavy torpedo tubes in favor of the lighter Mark XIII launching racks.

One other automatic weapons installation deserves mention here, this being the Elco-designed 'Thunderbolt'. Mounted in place of the 40 mm on the rear deck, the Thunderbolt was a power-driven armored turret mounting four 20 mm Oerlikon guns. An operator sat in the turret and trained the guns via a Mark 14 gunsight. PTs-556 through 559 were equipped with this installation and saw action in the Mediterranean. The system was primarily designed as an anti-aircraft weapon, and although possessed of a withering rate of fire, it was not overly effective against well armed F-lighters – against which even the 40 mm had little effect. On the few occasions suitable targets were found for the Thunderbolt, its performance was quite impressive. Again, had such a weapon been available with the early boats – and there is no reason why it could not have been, for the technology existed – PT Boats might well have chewed attacking Japanese aircraft to pieces at Pearl Harbor and in the Philippines.

Another weapon commonly carried by PT-Boats was the depth charge. Many boats were equipped with four or more depth charges, originally with the intention of using them against submarines. But the boats were not well suited for the task. The depth charges remained, however, when it was found that they were particularly useful in discouraging pursuing destroyers. On a number of occasions in the Solomons campaign depth charges were rolled overboard at a shallow setting to explode in front of a Japanese warship attempting to close one of the boats. Three hundred pounds of TNT was enough to break the back of a destroyer if it went off at the right moment.

A weapon of some usefulness to the PT-Boats in the Pacific was the field installation of an 81 mm mortar on the bow. By now the bow was becoming a rather crowded place, but a powerful mortar had its distinct uses. On approaching suspected enemy concentrations on islands where the dense jungle grew right down to the water, there was virtually no other weapon that could penetrate more than a few feet into the bush. A mortar solved that problem. Although it could also be used against barges, by the time a mortar found the range and managed to land a round aboard, the issue had probably already been settled in a blaze of automatic weapons fire. One other thing that mortars were good for, however, was when illumination of a target was desired: on numerous occasions, Japanese barges found themselves 'on the spot' with illumination from overhead.

During 1944 PT commands in both the Southwest Pacific and the Mediterranean began to experiment with barrage rocket installations on the boats. For the boats in Europe it was a desperate and futile effort to

come up with something that could deal with the heavily armored F-lighters. In the Pacific the weapon was intended more for bombardment of shore installations. Because the installations were cumbersome and the rockets rather inaccurate, the field experimentation was dropped.

The introduction of the five inch spin stabilized rocket with longer range and flatter trajectory brought a new lease of life to the idea of rocket-firing PT-Boats. In exhaustive tests conducted on the East Coast, the practicability of adding this weapon to the armament of the PT-Boat was investigated, and it was decided to equip new boats with two Mk 50 launchers giving a total salvo of sixteen rockets with one reload to be carried aboard. Although adding to the already heavy warload of the boats, the rockets gave the PTs a tremendous one-time punch that could, theoretically, put a destroyer out of commission. It was the promise of such tremendous firepower that prompted one official field report to conclude:

'Commander Motor Torpedo Boat Squadrons Seventh Fleet has requested that every rocket development be thoroughly investigated with a view to possible employment by PTs and that the development of a "motor rocket boat" be considered. If the present ratio of launcher to projector weight is maintained, and all PT armament except the turret twin fifties is removed, it would be possible to carry 5 tons of rocket equipment and deliver 4 tons of projectiles at the target at ranges in excess of 5,000 yards. This would

Right

Seen here are two particularly interesting photographs of Squadron 13 Higgins boats being buzzed by Army Air Force Bell P-39 Airacobras. The scenes would have taken place shortly after the squadron's commissioning and subsequent departure from New Orleans during November 1942 for what amounted to a 2500 mile grand tour of the Caribbean touching at Pensacola, Tampa, Key West, Cuba, Grand Cayman Island, Portland Bight, Jamaica, Barranquilla (Colombia) and finally on to the Panama Canal from where they would be shipped to Seattle prior to the squadron's duty in the Aleutians. The P-39s would probably be elements of the Caribbean Defense Command. PT-77 would serve long and well but would suffer an untimely end when she and PT-79 became the last two PT-boat losses of the war – at the hands of US gunners. On 1 February 1945, while patrolling off Mindoro in the Philippines, the two boats were taken under fire by a destroyer and destroyer escort that had wandered out of their assigned patrol area in search of targets. The two boats almost made good their getaway but the 77 ran aground at high speed on a reef. The 79, following behind the 77, turned hard to avoid the same fate only to take a direct shell hit and explode. Between the two crews, four men were killed while the remaining 30 crewmen all reached the shore of a nearby island.

give PTs tremendous firepower – greatly in excess of what they now have.

'The speed of rockets as compared with that of torpedoes should make them easier to hit targets with. With the development of radar on enemy ships, it may be more difficult to close them to a few hundred yards for a torpedo hit. Also the reliability of rockets would seem to be much greater than that of torpedoes and they will not require the same painstaking care. It is believed that all these advantages, plus the greater weight of explosive which can be delivered to the target, more than compensates for the torpedoes' single advantage of underwater destructive power.'

It is interesting to note that as early as this 1944 report naval men were envisioning the fast missile-armed patrol boats of today.

One other item of extreme usefulness, although not actually a weapon, was the smoke generator installed as standard on all PT-Boats. The generators were used in all sorts of situations, to fully cover a retirement, to hide the activities of landing craft and to protect other damaged boats. During night operations in the Solomons against the Tokyo Express, retiring boats often released puffs of smoke at which Japanese gunners seemed to enjoy firing. Early boats carried a standard United States Navy type generator consisting of a 35 gallon refillable tank secured to an emergency release carrier. Later in the war Elco developed their own generator, a non-refillable steel bottle which rested on wooden blocks and was held in place by two steel straps. A pipe with a nozzle at the end rose two feet from the bottle and spewed titanium tetrachloride which, when released into the atmosphere, formed a dense fog. The chemical reaction also produced caustic hydrochloric acid which dictated great care during operation and a thorough washing down of the stern after each use.

One last item of note which greatly increased the combat efficiency of the boats was the installation of radar. By late 1942 a few of the boats in the Solomons had been equipped experimentally with a version of an aircraft radar system, and although quite unreliable it demonstrated the great potential usefulness of the concept. Within a year special sets had been designed for use on the boats, and wholesale field modifications were in progress. On several occasions, primarily in the Mediterranean, successful torpedo attacks were carried out using radar bearings alone. In the Pacific radar greatly simplified the problem of locating and approaching Japanese barges, with the consequent unpleasant surprise to their occupants.

The very first Higgins squadron commissioned, Squadron 13, was assigned the most unpleasant task of duty in the Aleutians. After commissioning in September 1942 the squadron spent several months working up to strength and ironing out bugs in their new boats. PTs 73 through 84 ran from New Orleans to the Panama Canal on their own bottoms and then were shipped by freighter to Seattle during January 1943. From Seattle the boats proceeded to Adak, Alaska under their own power via Hardy Bay through the inland waterway, Bella Bella, Ketchikan, Juneay, Yukutat, Cordova, Kodiak, Sand Point, King Cove, Dutch Harbor and Atka. Right from the start, however, it was apparent that while the Higgins was a sturdy sea-going craft, it was also a very wet boat. Here a Higgins boat crosses another PT's wake during operations in the Aleutians.

PT-117

This series of ten photographs shows PT-117, fresh off the Elco production line, from virtually every angle. The boat is typical of the early 80 ft examples – the design and configuration of which came to be synonymous with the term PT-Boat. The boat is pictured, in these builder's photos, at rest and underway at speed. These photographs were taken on the day the boat was placed in service, 4 August 1942. One year to the month later, the 117, while serving with Squadron 6 in the Pacific, would be destroyed by enemy aircraft attacking Rendova Harbor.

1

2

3

4

5

8

9

10

58

Top Left
A fine view of the Higgins boat PT-78 cruising in Panamanian waters while in transit for the ultimate destination of the Aleutian Islands.

Top Right
One of Squadron 13's Higgins boats is unloaded from a cargo ship in Seattle in preparation for the run north to Alaska which would begin on 28 February 1943.

Center Right
Soon after the arrival of the Squadron 13 Higgins boats, which began their initial operations out of Finger Bay on Adak, American troops invaded Attu, the furthest island out in the chain, and after fierce ground fighting, gained control of the island from the Japanese defenders. The landings took place on 11 May 1943, and within one month a PT base had been installed at Casco Cove in Massacre Bay. PTs 75, 77, 79 and 82 were running patrols out of Attu by 4 June and were soon joined by two more Higgins boats of the newly arrived Squadron 16, PTs 219 and 224. But the Japanese High Command wrote off Attu, making no effort whatsoever to retake the island, and the PTs, once again, were denied any contact with the enemy. Three of Squadron 13's Higgins boats are seen in this photograph, dated 21 June 1943. The boats are tied up alongside the tender *Gillis* while a PBY refuels off the stern.

Bottom Right
After the Kiska landings the Amchitka PT base was abandoned after it was virtually destroyed by a severe storm. Finger Bay on Adak, however, remained an operational base for PT-Boats until May 1944, at which time the PT forces in the Aleutians were withdrawn. Seen in this photograph is the Finger Bay facility with PT tender *Tatoosh* anchored out in the deeper water. The Higgins boats did, at least, have forced-air heaters for use below decks so that men could actually live and function aboard.

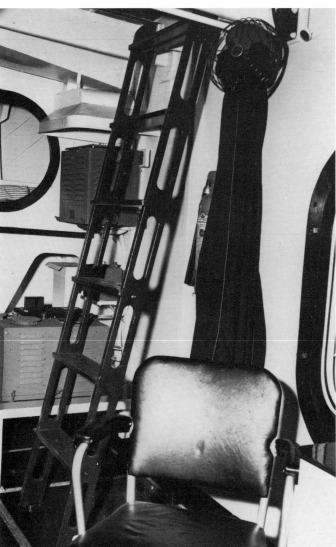

Top Left
Aboard a late-war Higgins 78-footer of the 625 class, this manufacturer's photo, taken at the time of launching, is from amidships looking forward toward the bridge. Ahead of the radar mast is the steel plate which serves as armor to protect the crew at the helm. The small arched cradle in the foreground supports the radar mast in its folded down position.

Top
A view of the bridge of a PT-625-class Higgins 78-footer. The arrangement was really quite spartan. The small devices into which the flexible cords extend are 'red lights' used to illuminate the instruments during night running.

Bottom Left
A view of a portion of the wardroom aboard a Higgins boat. The boat's waterline would be at approximately the floorline shown in this photo.

Top Right
This view shows part of the interior of the charthouse aboard a late-war Higgins boat. On the left is the radar console, and on the far right a portion of the boat's radio receiver is visible.

Bottom Right
The rudder and propeller arrangement on the underside of a Higgins 78-footer. Much experimentation was done throughout the war on the design of propellers, these being particularly sensitive items with respect to performance. Diameter and pitch had to be carefully matched to engine performance.

Top

Aboard a Higgins 78-footer, seen from between the two wing engines, this view is looking aft at the centerline mounted engine which was coupled to a V-drive unit. The two large black hoses extending from each side of the engine are the exhaust pipes which dump directly overboard on either side of the boat. Engine arrangement was somewhat similar on Elco boats, but the exhaust stacks were run all the way back to the stern where the exhaust could be routed through mufflers if so desired.

Bottom

Aboard the same 78 ft Higgins boat, we are now looking forward in the engine room from beside the rear centerline mounted engine. The two wing engines visible here drive straight through forward-neutral-reverse manually shifted transmissions. The large levers are the shifting handles. Orders to shift gears had to be piped down from the bridge. Understandably, the engine rooms of these boats had a tendency to become quite warm during operation.

Heading north through the inland passage of British Columbia was the most pleasurable period the crews would enjoy for some months to come. The conditions that awaited Squadron 13 in the Aleutians were nothing short of miserable.

Top Left

As a group of boats neared completion at the factory, the United States Navy would begin to assemble personnel at the construction site to form the nucleus of a new squadron. When the boats were completed and each had passed its trials, the squadron was then commissioned right at the factory. This photograph shows the commissioning ceremonies of Squadron 23 at the Higgins Industrial Canal Plant, New Orleans, on 28 June 1943. Note that these boats are still equipped with the old-style launching tubes.

Top Right

After nearly a year of enduring the foul Aleutian weather, it finally appeared in August 1943 that the PT forces based at Amchitka would get a crack at the enemy with the invasion of Kiska in the offing. Up to that point there had been utterly no contact with the enemy for any of the boats. B-24 bombers had been flying strikes on Kiska for some months, and it was believed that the invaders would have to deal with between 4,000 and 7,000 tough Japanese defenders. In an attempt to lessen the resistance at the actual landing sites, several Higgins boats were camouflaged as landing barges with orders to run up and down beaches several miles south of the actual landing zone in an effort to force the Japanese to deploy their troops needlessly. Alas, the 'bargized' PTs with phony painted soldiers peering over the sides did their job, even making several strafing runs close to the beach. But it all made little difference, for Kiska had been secretly and masterfully evacuated by the Japanese. The record of the PTs in the Aleutians would remain intact: no contact.

Center Right

Squadron 16 was sent to the Aleutians in August 1943 to reinforce Squadron 13. One of the Squadron 16 boats, PT-223, is seen here cutting across the wake of another boat during operations in the Aleutians. This boat, along with the remainder of the squadron, was later transferred to the South Pacific, seeing action at such bases as Mios Woendi, New Guinea, Mindoro in the Philippines and Brunei Bay, Borneo.

Bottom

Students at the PT training facility at Melville apply new planking to a war-weary PT-40 as part of their instruction on the care and repair of the wooden boats.

Top Left
The aft .50 caliber machine-gunner mans his twin Brownings on an 80 ft Elco boat. The mount was manually traversed by leg pressure in either direction from the gunner. In the background can be seen the boat's M-4 20 mm Oerlikon, this example mounted without a shield. The depression railing in front of the 20 mm mount keeps the gunner from shooting up his own boat in the excitement of combat.

Center Left
The Mark 4 20 mm cannon was an excellent weapon, but on the early PT-Boats this gun was installed on the stern complete with its heavy destroyer pedestal mounting and shield. Later PTs carried the gun mounted on a much lighter tripod arrangement, and when this weapon was moved up on to the port side of the bow to make room for a 40 mm gun on the stern, the tripod legs were shortened considerably to give the mount a lower profile.

Bottom Left
By strengthening the after deck area Elco was able to install a single 40 mm cannon on their boats, an arrangement which became standard and gave PTs a tremendous increase in firepower. Here sailors from the Melville training squadron prepare to practice-fire one of the weapons. Although originally designed as an anti-aircraft gun, the PT forces found it most useful in busting barges.

Top Right
All manner of weapons were field tested aboard PTs, beginning with the New Guinea campaign, in an effort to find a way of quickly dispatching armed Japanese barges before fire could be returned at PT attackers. Here crewmen test an anti-tank gun aboard an Elco 80-footer. Because such field pieces were manually loaded with one round at a time, their rate of fire was judged not to be high enough to be of much use.

Top
A view of the forward .50 caliber turret on the starboard side of an Elco 80-footer. This photo, taken aboard PT-149 in New Guinea, shows the small shock-absorbing mechanism built into the bottom of the gun mounts.

Bottom
A Higgins boat at speed in the English Channel. This boat, PT-199, happens to be carrying Admiral Harold R. Stark to the invasion beachhead during the D-day landings. A number of Higgins and Elco boats worked as escorts, shuttle boats and plane guards during the operation.

**Test launching of a Mark XIII torpedo with
exercise head (water filled) from one of the newly
devised launching racks. This torpedo and rack
installation came about as a result of the clear-cut
need to replace the Mark VIII and its associated
heavy steel tube. The origin of this rack can be
traced to a friendly conversation between two
boat skippers over drinks at a Manhattan bar in
February 1943.**

Left
**One of the Squadron 16 Higgins boats, PT-219, is
seen in this view at Kodiak, Alaska, while the
squadron was en route to the Aleutians. After
arriving at Attu PT-219 ran patrols for several
days but then suffered an unfortunate accident.
On 14 September a storm approached the island,
and although the 219 was tied to a buoy in Casco
Cove, winds gusting to 55 knots parted the
mooring line and drove the PT up on to the rocks.
The boat was pulled off but sank in twenty-five
feet of water. After the storm she was raised but
eventually scrapped.**

Top Left
Lt Bob Searles at the wheel of PT-564, the Higgins Hellcat, on which he briefly served as skipper for several test runs after his return from the early action in the Solomons.

Bottom Left
A sailor aboard an Aleutian-based Higgins PT prepares his twin .50 caliber machine-guns for the action that will never come. Note the covered cockpit modification made to this boat, testimony to the kind of weather conditions most often found in this theatre.

Top and Bottom Right
In early 1943 Higgins Industries conceived of their own initiative a new design for a PT-Boat. They constructed one example at their own expense which the United States Navy later purchased. Solomons veteran Bob Searles, who skippered the boat during its Navy trials periods, reported that the boat was superior in virtually every aspect of performance. The 70 ft Higgins 'Hellcat', numbered PT-564 could make 47 knots and could reverse course in nine seconds compared to twenty-two seconds for the standard 78 ft Higgins – which could itself run circles around an 80 ft Elco boat. Although expertly designed from a construction standpoint, which would have made it cheaper and easier to build, the Hellcat was never put into production. It was felt that the bigger boats then being built were more suited to the gunboat missions which were becoming more and more the forte of the PT-Boat.

Arming a PT-Boat with torpedoes was no easy
task, the process requiring hours of work both in
the torpedo shop and during the loading process.
This sequence of four photographs, taken in early
1942 at the Melville training center, shows PT-64
being armed with an exercise torpedo. The
process would have been much the same if not a
little slower, in a combat area.

In the first photograph, the weapon is
transported from the shop, after servicing and
preparation, to the dockside on a special cart. It is
hoisted from the cart and placed in racks on the
ground where (in the second photo) torpedomen
make depth and gyro adjustments. Note that the
torpedo is covered with a very heavy application
of grease and oil. In the third photograph, the
torpedo has been hoisted aboard the boat and,
using a special portable adjustable stand equipped
with rollers, the weapon is carefully inserted into
the heavy steel tube. The last photograph shows
the same torpedo being fired in a cloud of smoke
from the black powder charge. As can be seen
from this last photo, the clearance angle over the
deck was not great, and if a torpedo was launched
with an insufficient charge or if a partial misfire
occurred, the vanes of the torpedo often struck the
deck causing an erratic run.

Top
An engine is changed out of a Higgins boat at a
forward base in the Pacific. Engines could not be
overhauled in place: they had to be removed and
taken to a shop facility, usually in a rear area. The
1,350 hp Packard engine was as dependable as a
high-performance aviation engine could be. The
recommended life-cycle for the engine was 600
hours, but engines in combat areas often did
double their duty thanks to lack of replacement
parts – a condition that seemed to haunt PT
operations, often due to little more than bad luck.

Bottom
Detail view of the aft starboard torpedo tube
mounting on a 70 ft Elco boat. Note the lead screw
and track arrangement used to angle the tube out
into firing position. The device on the top at the
end of the tube contained the black powder charge
used to launch the torpedo.

Top

Aboard a New Guinea-based Elco 80-footer, a torpedoman demonstrates the method used to crank out the torpedo tubes to the correct firing angle. Note the positive lock at the nose of the tube. The crank handle was normally stowed on the roof of the dayroom cabin amidships.

Bottom

Details of an early .50 caliber installation on an Elco 77-footer. Later the entire mounting and carriage system was revamped, moving the ammo boxes on to shelves within the turret.

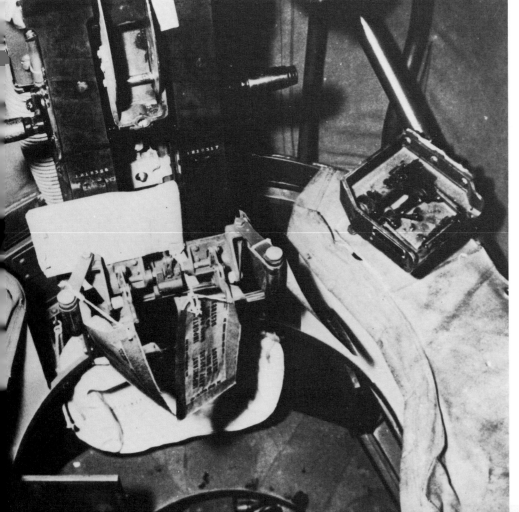

Top Left
Two different worlds. The top photograph shows an example of the World War One-vintage Mark VIII destroyer torpedo. It was about all the United States Navy had to offer its PT forces in the early stages of the war. The price paid for such obsolescence was very high. In contrast, the lower picture shows an example of the later Mark XIII aircraft torpedo which eventually came to be standard equipment on late war boats. Requiring a light-weight rack from which the weapon was simply rolled into the sea, the Mark XIII offered increased performance, greater reliability and more hitting power than the Mark VIII. Comparative lengths were 20 ft 6 in. for the Mark VIII and 13 ft 6 in. for the Mark XIII.

Bottom Left
A view rarely seen in photos of PT-Boats is what the inside of one of the .50 caliber gun tubs looked like. Special circular ammo cans were locked into place in the tubs on either side of the gunner.

Top Right
A factory-installed 37 mm gun in action off the coast of New Guinea during 1944. A target on the beach has been set afire by rounds from the cannon.

Bottom Right
A view of a field-installed 37 mm gun on the bow of an Elco 80-footer in New Guinea. This gun was originally designed for installation in the nose of the Army P-39 fighter plane. PT crews found that its light weight made it ideal for use aboard their boats and offered the kind of punch necessary to deal with Japanese barge traffic. Here two crewmen load their weapon with explosive shells.

Top

A view of a 40 mm installation on a late-war Elco 80-footer. This boat also displays the revamped engine hatch found on late production boats which replaced several of the ventilators with a single, large forward-facing air scoop which brought fresh air into the engine room.

Bottom

A close look at an Elco Thunderbolt unit on the dock at Bayonne, New Jersey prior to lifting aboard a boat. The mounting consisted mainly of a power-driven turret, four Oerlikon 20 mm guns and an operator's seat position. The weapon may well have been inspired by a similar Rheinmetal-Borsig quad flak 20 mm originally developed for truck-mounted anti-aircraft use by the German Army but often mounted aboard German E-boats (S-Boats) with which the PTs frequently tangled in the Mediterranean. The obvious advantage of this type of weapon was its tremendous (for the time) rate of fire.

Top

A depth charge dropped in the path of a pursuing destroyer discouraged more than one Japanese skipper from pressing home his attack on a fleeing PT-Boat. The desired effect could usually be achieved with a depth setting of about 100 feet.

Bottom

All sorts of schemes were tested to improve and add to the firepower of the PT-Boat throughout the war, primarily in answer to the problem of dealing with heavily armed barges. Here a sailor prepares to test fire a field-contrived weapon consisting of six bazooka launchers strapped together and mounted on a tripod. The boat is an Elco 80-footer with an early type radar installation.

Top Left
An Elco 80-footer displays the use of its smoke generator. The 35-gallon bottles mounted on the stern expelled titanium tetrachloride which billowed into thick white fog when released into the atmosphere. In the early Solomons battles these smoke generators came in handier than anyone dreamed when it was decided to add the item to the boats' equipment.

Bottom Left
A view of a PT-Boat smoke generator shows the method in which the 35 gallon tanks were secured to the deck. With a few turns of a wrench, the tanks could be quickly discarded overboard, a tactic used on at least one occasion in the Solomons to decoy the enemy to a floating generator while the PT in question made good its escape.

Top Right
By 1945 the familiar radar dome atop the mast of virtually every PT-Boat then in service became a second-class piece of equipment with the introduction of a new type of improved radar designed specifically for use aboard the boats. As seen in this photograph, the mast arrangement was somewhat more streamlined, being developed by Elco for use on their production line beginning with PT-565.

Bottom Right
Although the hull is exactly the same as that introduced with PT-103, the first Elco 80-footer, these three late-war boats offer silhouettes totally foreign to those first boats of 1942, thanks to a tremendous increase in the equipment and weaponry carried aboard. Equipped with 20 mm, 37 mm, 40 mm and .50 caliber guns as well as Mark XIII torpedoes and radar, the boats pack more punch per ton of displacement than any other vessel in the United States Navy.

Top Left and Right, Bottom Left
During late 1942/early 1943 while the Bureau of Ships attempted to develop effective camouflage schemes for PT-Boats, Elco was directed to apply a 'zebra' pattern to PT-170. This pattern was later field tested in the combat zones. Other than attention, nothing overly remarkable was gained with the scheme. Obviously the intent was to confuse the enemy as to the type of craft, its size and direction of travel. Concealment was *not* one of the pattern's strongpoints.

Bottom Right
To the pilot of a fast-moving Allied fighter or bomber one small boat often looked like another, and there were several instances of Allied aircraft attacking PT-Boats with tragic results. To further minimize the possibility of such occurrences, these Higgins boats – seen here tied up at the Bastia base – have had large white stars painted on their bows. Note the varying installations of 37 mm cannons removed from the noses of Army P-39 fighters.

5
The Solomons Test

'For over a year we had practised complex squadron maneuvers . . . formation running, squadron attack dispositions and tactics . . . almost all of it in the daylight. Now here we were, four boats heading out into the black of night, getting separated, without the slightest idea of _how_ we were going to _find_ the enemy, let alone pull off an attack.'

(Robert L. Searles talking about the first PT attack on Japanese warships in the Solomons, 12 October, 1942.)

'Conservative Offensive' was the kind of official terminology bandied about by planners. It characterized those landings that took place on Guadalcanal Island in the Solomons chain during early August 1942. After the attack on Pearl Harbor the Japanese had moved in a dozen directions in the Pacific, invading scores of islands and territories, sometimes opposed and sometimes not. Everywhere but in the Philippines what opposition there was quickly crumbled.

With the surrender of Corregidor in May 1942 the Japanese put into high gear a major operation aimed at Port Moresby, New Guinea. Simply stated, the plan was to isolate Australia by putting Japanese airfields within striking distance of the Allied shipping lanes to Australia and New Zealand. The attempted invasion resulted in the first important Japanese setback in the Battle of the Coral Sea. While this first major sea battle was a tactical draw, it was a strategic victory for the United States and her allies, the Japanese invasion fleet having been forced to turn back despite inflicting considerable damage on American ships. The following month, however, brought the Battle of Midway, a resounding and clear-cut United States victory.

Defensive victories were one thing; but after such good fortune at Midway, American planners decided to strike at the enemy in a way he least expected at the time. It would be a bold amphibious operation aimed at regaining the southern tip of the Solomons. The move would have to be premature to be certain, for there were precious few ships in the area to back up such an operation in the event of interference and counter-attacks by powerful Japanese surface and air

elements. While the Japanese had lost a big chunk of their carrier force at Midway, they still had scores of battleships and cruisers on hand, not to mention a destroyer force second to none in the world. But the best defense is often a good offense, and it was reasoned that such an invasion of 'Japanese territory' might busy the enemy to the extent that he would at least forget about any further expansion in the area.

A look at a map of the Solomon Islands will make it obvious why it was planned right from the beginning to use PT-Boats in the area. Numerous jungle islands, large and small, with narrow seas between, looked as though they would be happy hunting grounds for hordes of torpedo-firing mosquito boats. Unfortunately, there were no hordes of boats to be had. Since the beginning of the war, however, PT-Boat Squadron 2 had been operating in the Panama Sea Frontier in protection of United States interests there. The Squadron, equipped with 77 ft Elco boats, had been growing steadily in numbers through the Spring and Summer of 1942. In the factories back home Elco had completed their contract for the 77-footers and were now producing a new 80 ft design, a much improved boat. But trained squadrons of these boats would not be ready for months. Higgins, too, was finally into production on a 78 ft model, but if the Navy was going to get a force of PT-Boats into the Guadalcanal area before the issue became academic, it would have to send the 77 ft Elco boats that had been training for just such a chance under balmy Panamanian skies.

The oversized Squadron 2 – consisting of fourteen boats by July – was ordered to break off eight craft to be designated as a new

Squadron 3 which would prepare for immediate deployment to the South Pacific. The invasion was only a month away. Of course no one within the PT commands had any idea what was planned, but it looked like action was close at hand and all were anxious to prove the worth of their boats in combat.

By August, the month of the invasion, all was ready in Panama. The first four boats of the new squadron, PTs 38, 46, 48 and 60, were loaded aboard cargo ships which sailed for points south on the 29th, arriving mid September at the rear area of Noumea, New Caledonia. One of the Squadron 3 skippers, a man who would distinguish himself in combat, Henry Stillman 'Stilly' Taylor of PT-46, later commented on the arrival of this first group of PTs in the war zone:

'Everything was snafu when the first section reached a rear base in the South Pacific. Apparently no one had figured soon enough how they were going to get the boats off the ships. Those boats weighed 50 tons. When we arrived, the SeaBees were working on a huge floating crane, and still it was three weeks before the boats got into the water. No one seemed to know where we were supposed to go, where our base would be. We had to wait – and so did the Marines [suffering on Guadalcanal] – for the admirals to make up their minds.

'We heard about how the Japs were coming down [the Slot] every night and shelling Guadalcanal, and we talked about how we would sink the whole Jap fleet. The Japs were starting down from an island called Bougainville, so we used to say "We'll derail the Bougainville Express". We were pretty cocky then.'

By the time the boats of the first division

Top
A 77-foot Elco of Squadron 3 caught in the early morning sun. Note the canvas covers over the twin .50 caliber machine-guns to protect the mechanisms from salt spray.

Right
Early Elco 77-footers cruise in column off the east coast during 1941. These boats would soon be on their way to Panama, and then on to the Solomon Islands to do battle with the 'Tokyo Express'. In the foreground is the port aft torpedo tube covered with canvas and the end of the port forward tube with its black powder cylinder afixed on top.

These two photographs show Elcos of the training squadron entering the Net and Boom Depot at Melville, Rhode Island and tying up alongside the tender *Jamestown*. A number of the boats seen here were reassigned within a year so that newer and different types could be brought in for crew and personnel familiarization training.

had been unloaded and had been towed to the island of Espiritu Santo by their newly arrived tender the *Jamestown*, the second division, consisting of PTs 37, 39, 45 and 61, was en route from Panama aboard a merchant ship destined for the first PT-Boat base in the South Pacific, Tulagi Harbor, only thirty-five miles across the bay from the ground fighting on Guadalcanal. The second division would arrive on 25 October, but not before the first four boats had tasted combat.

As the first division of Squadron 3 pulled into Tulagi Harbor under their own power on the morning of 12 October, not fifty miles away heavy American surface units were engaging like Japanese elements in what would be but another in a long series of fiercely contested sea battles in the area, this one later being termed by historians the Battle of Cape Esperance. Both sides would suffer heavy losses throughout this campaign, in this particular case the United States Navy was giving better than it was getting, but the cruisers *Salt Lake City* and *Boise* were hit and in need of repair, not to mention the loss of the destroyer *Duncan*. These were losses the Navy could ill afford, for the Japanese were far superior in terms of numbers of ships available, and although United States surface forces sortied for battle as often as they could, during the early months of the campaign the Japanese would send ships into what would become known as 'Iron Bottom Sound' to roam about unopposed and shell the Marines desperately holding on to Henderson Airfield on Guadalcanal while the outnumbered American destroyers and cruisers patched their wounds in rear areas. There just weren't enough ships on hand to meet the Japanese every night; but the four newly arrived PT-Boats of Squadron 3 helped even the odds just a little.

The boat crews spent the days of 12 and 13 October setting up their advance base as best they could. Tired from two days of hard work, the crews retired on the night of the 13th only to be awakened at 2.00 am the following morning by the boom of heavy gunfire not far away. Every man knew what the bright orange flashes in the distance meant. Marines huddled together in foxholes on Guadalcanal were dying amidst the whine of fourteen-inch shells, and the Japanese aboard those big ships out in the bay were perhaps just a little complacent in their belief that no one could do anything to stop them.

According to Lt Cmdr Alan R. Montgomery, squadron commander for the four newly arrived boats: 'We got word the afternoon of the thirteenth that a Japanese task force was 'in the Slot' and moving down toward us. Apparently it consisted of three

destroyers, or a cruiser and two destroyers. Patrol planes had spotted them and the word was passed along to us.

'When I heard it, I went at once to General Rupertus (commander of the Marine forces on Tulagi) to find out what he thought about it. I told him I didn't consider it wise to sacrifice our number one weapon of surprise on so small an enemy. No fooling – that's what I told him. It will give you some idea of what we thought of those boats of ours.

'The general agreed that we should wait for something really worthwhile. He smiled as he said it. Now that I look back on that little conversation, I realize why he was smiling; but at the time there was nothing very droll to me in the idea of four midget PT-boats haughtily refusing to attack a trio of Japanese destroyers because they weren't big enough.'

Later in the day Montgomery flew over to Guadalcanal in a Grumman 'Duck' amphibian biplane to consult with the Marine commanders on the island. On the way back down to the airplane, he could not help but notice the reception he and his party were receiving from the Marine troops they encountered.

'Remember, those boys had been taking all the Japs could send at them since 7 August, without reprieve. When they found out that our squadron, or half squadron, of motor torpedo boats had come in to work with them, they may have felt that here at last was recognition, however small, for the job they'd done. They hadn't been forgotten after all.

'But mostly they were thinking of those damned Jap ships that slipped down the Slot at night to shell them. They had an amazing string of unprintable names for that nocturnal annoyance, and were counting on us to do something about it. I remember one haggard, red-eyed youngster who came up to me with a Jap knife stuck in his belt and said, "Just teach the bastards to stay home in bed nights where they belong. Just do that, and we'll remember you in our prayers".'

'I hoped we could do it.'

The rumbling explosions coming across 'Sleepless Lagoon', the stretch of water between Tulagi and Guadalcanal so-called by the Marines because of the incessant shelling that came from its waters, were clearly not being made by any three destroyers. There were heavy ships out there, targets definitely befitting the PTs' attention.

'I ordered all boats to get underway immediately and then sent word to General Rupertus that "this was it" and we were going out', according to Montgomery.

The squadron commander was highly respected by everyone under his command. He was regular navy while all of the

squadron's other officers were drawn from reservist volunteers. Montgomery understood his men and got along well with them. Despite a serious case of pneumonia contracted during the trip from Panama, he was determined to go along on this first show. Thin and gaunt from his illness and covered from head to foot with painful waterblisters as a result of taking so much sulphur, he was not about to miss his first chance to strike at the enemy, and rode along in PT-60 as overall tactical commander with the boat's skipper Lt John 'Jack' Searles. Jack's brother Robert had PT-38, PT-48 was skippered by Lt Robert Wark and Lt Stilly Taylor commanded the 46 boat.

With PT-60 in the lead, the boats moved out of Tulagi Harbor in a column. A dozen 1,200 hp Packards rumbled low across the water. With their muffler systems engaged, the boats opened up to about 20 knots. The men took long deep breaths to ease the nervousness they felt. This was what many of them had been training for for over a year and a half. This was what they had come for.

'Clearing Tulagi Harbor there were the four of us', according to Montgomery, 'and at first we maintained contact with one another. That didn't last long, however. In the dark we soon lost touch, and you had a feeling of aloneness that sat in your throat like an egg.'

As Stilly Taylor later put it, 'We had trained and been on many practice runs at night, but there had never been anything like this. We found out later that the Japanese would typically wait for the darkest overcast nights to make their runs. Running by ourselves, we really had no idea *how* we were going to find and torpedo Japanese ships in the black of night.'

About half way across the sound, the crews could plainly see the bright orange flashes of the heavy Japanese guns. While it gave the boats a direction in which to head, it also ruined the night vision of the men aboard.

After a run of about twenty minutes, the four boats – now virtually independent of each other in the black of the night – were closing the enemy formation. But with only the gun flashes as a guide, the skippers had no real idea of where they were or what the composition of the enemy force might be. Stilly Taylor recalled later, 'PT-Boats should have been manned by cats. They might have been able to see what was going on that night. We couldn't. All we could see was the flash of gunfire in a tight formation which was moving down from Cape Esperance to Lunga Point at about 20 knots, swinging out and around and back again – and the tracers arching ashore.'

Just as the PTs drew close, all but one of

the Japanese ships stopped firing, their bombardment mission apparently completed. As the crews peered ahead into the black night hoping to line up a battleship or one of the cruisers, they had no way of knowing they were penetrating a screening force of some eight Japanese destroyers – but they soon found out.

As the action began, all four boats were still heading in the same approximate direction – toward the Guadalcanal shore – but were now widely separated. PT-60 had unknowingly penetrated the destroyer screen and was lining up on the last cruiser still firing at the shore. PTs 46 and 48 were several thousand yards behind PT-60 and off to its right. The 46 and 48 were less than 100 yards apart, but neither skipper was fully aware of the other's position as the two boats unknowingly approached the destroyer screen. Bob Searles in PT-38 had become completely separated from the main group, ending up several miles to the east.

The action that night was extremely confusing. Although the official battle action reports leave certain questions unanswered, it has been possible, through additional

interviews, to piece together at least the opening moments of the action with some degree of accuracy. The reader must bear in mind, however, that in the black of night, everyone is blind. The only men who could ever relate this story were the men who were there, and none had ever been in action before. It is perhaps a little too much to ask of a boy aged twenty-two, under fire for the first time in his life, to recall bearings, sequences, silhouettes and events with any degree of accuracy, especially from the deck of a bouncing motor boat in the midst of a wild free-for-all. Much of the testimony is conflicting in this case – just as with later actions. Postwar testimony from Japanese sources did virtually nothing to clear up any of the questions as to who did what and who hit what. Such assessments did not even confirm damage or sinkings, but this is not surprising as the Japanese were often prone to exaggerating victories and ignoring losses even in their official reports. But as nearly as can be determined, here is what happened:

PT-60 continued to sneak in on its cruiser target. With engines still muffled, Montgomery conned the wooden boat to within

Aboard PT-61 during the period this boat was based at New York. An officer works the throttles while an enlisted man has the helm. Under the command of Lt Hugh Robinson, commander of Squadron 3 in the Solomons, this boat would go up against the 'Tokyo Express'.

400 yards of the hulking vessel. Montgomery later recalled machinist's mate Tubby Kiefer turning to gunner's mate Teddy Kuharski and asking, 'Gee, Ski. Ain't that the *Boise*?' It was not the *Boise*.

Unlike her three sister boats, PT-60 carried only two torpedoes, depth charges originally having been installed in place of the aft two tubes during the days when it was hoped that PT-Boats could also be used effectively against submarines. Searles squared up the boat with the cruiser right in front of him, cut the throttles, and in the same instant hit the two firing buttons. He then unbaffled the exhaust pipes and poured on the power, swinging the 60 Boat hard left to make his escape. Now making better than 40 knots on a heading back for Tulagi, all hands on the bridge watched two dull red explosions shoot into the air at the cruiser's waterline. The men had seen what the big ship's gun flashes looked like, having watched them all the way over, and the explosions they saw were not guns firing. Montgomery and Searles were certain they had hit the cruiser.

'And right there', Montgomery later testified, 'we got the surprise of our sweet young lives. We were running wide open when Jack Searles, who was always thinking of his engines, said ever so casually, "We can slow down now, Commander. They didn't spot us" – and he eased back on the throttles.

'I didn't have a chance to answer him. A salvo of enemy fire burst around our ears, and we were damn near blown off the boat. Jack and I both jammed the throttles wide, practically up through the windshield, and the PT went soaring. What had happened – in turning from the cruiser we had run smack into the whole hornet's nest of destroyers.'

PT-60 had indeed run into the midst of the screening destroyers. One of the Japanese escorts flicked on its searchlight, catching the PT-Boat fully in its powerful beam and providing yet another destroyer with a perfect silhouette at which to fire. But he was unaware that the skipper of the Japanese destroyer was about to cut two PT-Boats in half when he turned on his light.

Stilly Taylor was still groping about in the darkness in PT-46, looking for something to shoot at, when suddenly the searchlight beam blazed on just ahead of him. At one end

The entrance to the living area at the Tulagi PT base looked like something out a Hollywood movie. As seen from out on the floating dock, the sign over the entrance to the compound reads 'CALVERTVILLE. Through these portals pass the best MTB flotilla in the world'. The village was so named in honor of Cmdr Allen P. Calvert, Commander Motor Torpedo Boat Flotilla 1.

Right
Lt Commander Alan R. 'Monty' Montgomery led the first Squadron 3 strike against the enemy on the night of 13–14 October 1942. Well liked by his men, Montgomery had to be relieved of his command before the squadron's next combat, thanks to a severe case of pneumonia contracted on the voyage to the South Pacific.

of the beam he could clearly make out a PT-Boat. At the other end he could see the hulking outline of a ship, now only a few yards away, bearing directly down on him. Taylor opened the throttles wide and swung his boat hard right.

Bob Wark in PT-48 also saw the searchlight, saw the enemy destroyer bearing down on him and then, an instant later, saw Stilly Taylor cut directly in front of him passing from left to right. Reacting quickly, Wark cut the throttles, allowing Taylor to squeeze through the gap between the 48 Boat and the destroyer, then applied full power and spun the wheel to the right in an effort to save his own boat. He continued to hold the rudder hard over and, as radioman Woodrow Cavanah later pointed out, 'I thought Mr. Wark was just going to turn a complete circle and come right back in for a torpedo run. It happened that way on a number of occasions later. You'd be out looking for trouble and you wouldn't know you'd found a Japanese ship until you almost rammed him, and then you were too close for a torpedo attack. So you'd turn back out, circle around and head in for a firing run only to find that you now couldn't locate the target. That's the way it was before radar.'

But Wark didn't hold the rudder hard right for long. He turned the 48 through 180° – a half circle – and then suddenly swung the wheel around putting the boat into a hard left turn through 90°. PT-48 was now running flat out on a course approximately parallel to the Guadalcanal coast heading west, the same course as the Japanese ships heading for home back up the Slot. Very shortly the murky outline of yet another Japanese destroyer was spotted off the starboard side. Judged to be about 200 yards away and running a parallel course to that of the 48 boat, she apparently had not spotted the boiling phospherescent wake of the speeding PT. Wark did not wish to be pinned between the shore and an angry destroyer and determined that the first order of business was to put himself on the other side of the speeding Japanese ship. Rather than turn in and attempt to cut across her wake, Wark elected to run up far enough ahead of the destroyer so as to be able to cut to the right across her bow. As Woodrow Cavanah later recalled, 'Why Mr Wark decided to cut in front of that destroyer I'll never know. But we sure cut it close.'

Quartermaster Crumpton made a special point to instruct both of the .50 caliber turret gunners to hold their fire unless spotted. He realized that at this close range the destroyer would probably cut the 48 into matchsticks if they were detected, and he told gunner's mate Merwin Todd and the other turret gunner – who shall go unnamed – not to open fire on the destroyer unless she opened fire first. When Wark judged the PT far enough ahead of the speeding destroyer, he made his move. Zipping across the ship's bow, the 48 remained, incredibly, undetected. As the PT pulled around to the other side of the destroyer, a searchlight suddenly flicked on. According to radioman Cavanah:

'They probed around and passed right over us, continuing its sweep. That's when this nineteen-year-old gunner – he was a kid we had picked up in Panama as a replacement – opened up from his .50 caliber turret. That

Life at Tulagi was something short of an idyllic South Seas setting. Part of the living quarters are visible in this R.L. Searles photo.

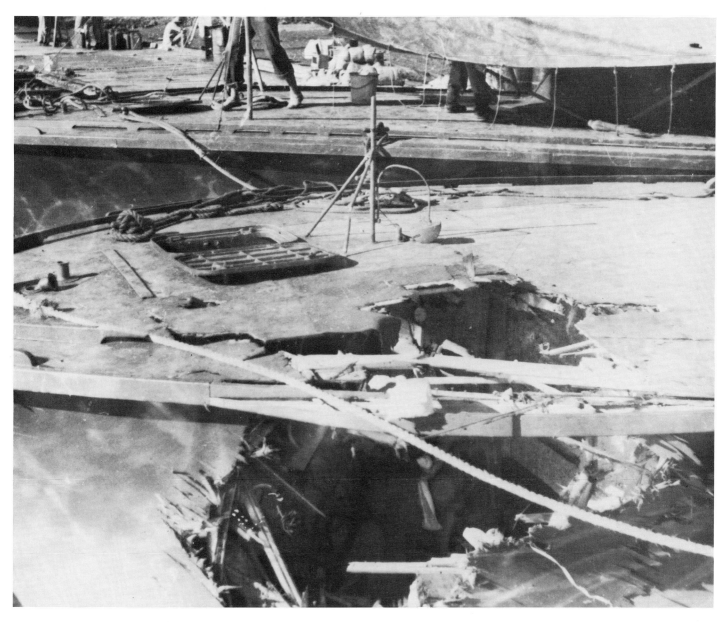

searchlight zipped right back over and pinpointed us, and I swear I could feel it burning the back of my neck. Why that kid did what he did I'll never know, but that was, far as I know, the last time he rode one of our squadron's PT-Boats. When that light hit us, I figured we were really in for it. Almost immediately three 4.7 in. shells landed *very* close to us, one to port, one to starboard, and the last right in our wake. That's when 'ol Todd opened up from the other .50 caliber turret. They say cooks make good gunners and they were sure right about Todd. He was just as cool as could be. He poured a burst into that searchlight, and we were so close to that ship that we could all hear the glass exploding and shattering above the gunfire and the roar of the engines.'

When the searchlight went out all firing stopped. The destroyer had apparently had

enough, and the streaking PT was headed for home. Wark continued on for some minutes, and then realizing he had no idea where he was, shut the boat down. Feeling that he was far enough away from the action, he decided to drift until first light when he could head for home. As Cavanah put it, 'Mr Wark took some booze he had stored away and passed it around – but I felt too sick to drink'.

Aboard PT-46, after having narrowly squeaked between the onrushing destroyer and PT-48, Stilly Taylor swung back on to his original course in towards Guadalcanal, still hoping to find one of the bigger ships that had, by now, stopped firing. Unable to do so, he roared about the sound for a while longer, hunting targets to no avail. First light found him, like Wark, drifting about waiting for a hint as to how to get back to Tulagi.

When PT-60 was caught full in the search-

After three PTs attacked three Japanese destroyers off Guadalcanal on the night of 8–9 November 1942, the boats turned and streaked for home. But a well-placed Japanese 4.7 in. shell caught squadron commander Hugh Robinson's PT-61 in the bow, blowing a large hole in the boat. By keeping the damaged PT on a plane, Robinson managed to get the boat back to Tulagi. Next morning the squadron leader snapped this photograph of his damaged craft.

light of the destroyer that was bearing down on PTs 46 and 48, she immediately began taking fire from another destroyer off to starboard. Both the DDs quickly fell into line, determined to give chase to the 60 and settle the matter. As Montgomery recalled, after being spotted and taken under fire, 'Everybody ducked. Later we all got a good laugh out of that because, of course, there is nothing on a PT-Boat to duck behind.

'As we took off in the general direction of Tulagi, there were two destroyers on our tail. Enemy shells, mostly 4.7s, screamed around us like rockets, and the gun flashes were so continuous that they seemed to light up the whole place like daylight.'

PT-60 was making full speed, zigzagging wildly through the night to evade the heavy shells now falling uncomfortably close. Montgomery ordered the smoke generator turned on, and as the billowy white fog began to pour out a shell landed squarely in the 60's wake almost lifting the boat out of the water. Torpedoman Willie Uhl picked himself up off the deck and returned to his post at the smoke generator. Soon the leading destroyer was in the smoke and, according to Montgomery, 'We could see his tracers streaking by us – small red balls of fire, some of which seemed to hang suspended in space for an incredibly long time as they passed us. Those Japs were good gunners but they couldn't locate us, nor could they see where the shells were falling.'

Montgomery then ordered the boat's depth charges dropped over the side. It was a clever move, for whether the Japanese thought there were other torpedo boats around or perhaps that they had run into a minefield, or whether they had correctly guessed what

Montgomery was up to, they abandoned the chase. Such an underwater explosion beneath a destroyer's hull could put the ship out of commission and the prize just wasn't worth it. Just in case, Montgomery ordered the smoke generator dumped overboard, hoping to trick the enemy into thinking the boat had gone down while the PT made good its escape.

'Looking back', said Montgomery, 'we could make out the dim shapes of the two destroyers nosing around the spot where we had jettisoned the smoke pots.

'Our plan was to slip around Florida and hole up in the first safe hiding place until daylight, when the Japs would go home. It seemed the wisest thing to do, because Sleepless Lagoon was full of Japs, and any attempt to go through them, back to our Tulagi base, might be suicidal.

'So at slow speed, ghosting along with every man alert for more trouble, we felt our way past the Florida shore – and suddenly found the way blocked by a destroyer lying to across Sandfly Passage. Apparently he was doing sentry work for the force which had come steaming into the channel.

'There we were, and there he was, and the only thing we could do was cut our engines, sit tight, and send up a fervent ten-man prayer

Top
Motor mechanics labor over a Packard 1,200 hp V-12 engine aboard an Elco 77-footer based at Tulagi Harbor. With no forced ventilation unless the boats were moving, life in the engine room tended to be on the warm side. It was a credit to the training and ingenuity of the mechanics who manned the engine rooms that they should have such an excellent overall record in terms of boat availability while facing the very difficult task of trying to make high performance gasoline-powered engines perform under extremely difficult conditions.

Top Right
A view of the entrance to the Tulagi machine shop. There was little need to pick up trash, which generally stayed where it was first dropped. The large dark crate in the center of the photo contains a Packard replacement engine.

Bottom Right
Within the Tulagi machine shop, the best was done with what few spare parts were on hand. Two men are busy here overhauling a Packard engine.

Six of the PT-Boat skippers involved in the wild actions off Guadalcanal in late 1942: from the rear, left to right, Lt Jack Searles, Lt Tom Kendall and Lt Charles Tilden. Bottom row, left to right, Lt Robert Searles, Lt 'Stilly' Taylor and Lt Leonard Nikoloric.

that he would not discover our presence.'

There were long hard moments ahead for the 60. Her only two torpedoes expended, there was nothing she could do to harm the sitting-duck destroyer. It was as irritating as it was frightening, but shortly before dawn the Japanese destroyer departed leaving the men of PT-60 to breathe a long, deep sigh of relief. 'We started our engines', recalled Montgomery, 'and discovered to our complete disgust that we were stuck fast. The bottom there was coral, wickedly sharp, and the ebbing tide had dropped us on the reef.'

PT-60 was finally spotted the following afternoon and hauled off the rocks, her bottom so badly damaged that it would be many weeks before she was serviceable again.

When the action began, it will be recalled that Bob Searles in PT-38 was several miles to the east and generally out of touch with the whole affair. But he soon ran into his own trouble. A searchlight from a Japanese destroyer flicked on, swept right over the 38 and then went off again, the destroyermen apparently satisfied that they were in no immediate danger. Moments later what Searles estimated to be a light cruiser loomed up ahead. Engines still muffled, PT-38 closed the target, which appeared to be heading back up the Guadalcanal shore for her home at Bougainville. At 400 yards, Searles fired the two aft torpedoes, one of which cleared its tube only to strike its fins on the deck of the PT. The second torpedo never left its tube, but hung precariously overboard, its engine melting itself in a hot run and setting up a tremendous racket. The men at the torpedo shop back on Tulagi quickly learned from such experiences that more black powder was needed for a clean launch in the humid South Pacific climate, but Bob Searles was stuck with his fate this night. While torpedomen worked feverishly to stop the hot running torpedo, Searles continued on in toward the still unsuspecting cruiser. At 200 yards he launched his two forward fish, only to have one of *those* stick in the tube. But the fourth torpedo got away clean, and at this range it could hardly miss. With his last torpedo in the water, Searles opened the exhaust baffles and the throttles at the same time, intending to pass close astern of his target. As they skipped over the cruiser's wake, all hands on deck felt a heavy underwater explosion. Searles looked back to see a red glow at the cruiser's waterline, forward of the bridge. The first explosion was followed immediately by a secondary explosion.

PT-38 laid smoke and headed for home, the cruiser having stopped firing after being torpedoed. After running for some minutes, Searles also cut his engines and drifted until

first light, only to find that he was not far off Tulagi Harbor. As a result of the hot runs, one of the torpedoes had actually welded itself to its tube, and as Searles later recalled, 'The next day the chief torpedoman back at the base disarmed the boat while we all watched . . . from a hill about a hundred yards away.'

This first wild mêlé was a perfect example of what was in store for the boats of Squadron 3. We have gone into considerable detail on this first action as it was a shining example of the way the motor torpedo boat weapons system concept worked in reality rather than theory. On this night the PTs had perhaps the most important element in all battles working for them – surprise. Never again would they enjoy the benefit of this factor. Creating mass confusion in the night would be their trademarks, but even with the element of surprise on their side the PTs ended up as confused in the darkness as the ships they stalked. This, too, would be typical. The results of this first action remain unclear to this day. The examination of postwar records did not help, but it is interesting to note that Radio Tokyo announced, shortly after the attack, that one of its task forces had been attacked by nineteen torpedo boats, twelve of which had been destroyed against the loss of one cruiser. Radio Tokyo rarely admitted losses and generally down-played those it did admit to.

The battle for the lower Solomons would have two distinct phases. From August through November 1942 the Japanese would hotly contest the issue with every intention of annihilating the invaders. Several major naval operations combined with heavy troop reinforcement efforts were mounted, each one bigger than its predecessor and each one failing to dislodge the tenacious American Marines with their prized Henderson Field. Finally, during mid-November, the enemy threw everything they had into an effort that would come to be known as the Sea Battle of Guadalcanal during which the Japanese would suffer heavy losses to American warships as well as aircraft. These were sea battles the likes of which had never been seen for their ferocity and destructiveness. Virtually all the surface actions were fought at night, and as often as possible the PT-Boats from Tulagi were out poking about Iron Bottom Sound, trying their best to get into the midst of things, hoping to pick up the slack for the still outnumbered capital ships of the United States Navy.

With their losses in mid-November 1942 the Japanese had in fact conceded that theater to the Allies, whose operations now clearly switched from defense in the form of protect-

ing a marginal invasion force, to offense. The task at hand was clear and simple – to eradicate the Japanese from the Southern Solomons, and then keep on going. But by then it was the turn of the Japanese to be tenacious and their forces would continue to battle on Guadalcanal for three more hellish months, being supplied all the while by what would come to be known as the infamous 'Tokyo Express' led by possibly the finest Japanese naval commander of World War Two, Rear Admiral Raizo Tanaka. Here, too, the PT-Boats from Tulagi would be heavily involved. Having grown considerably in strength of numbers by this time, they would achieve commendable successes and suffer some of their worst losses against Tanaka's deadly destroyers.

* * * * * *

After that first hectic action of 13–14 October the outlook for the Allied forces in the Guadalcanal area grew progressively worse. The following night the Japanese sent cruisers down the Slot to bombard the hapless Marines, and once again the Marines could do nothing but dig in and bear it. PTs 38 and 60 were unserviceable and PTs 46 and 48 had been sent on a mission to escort a 'Yippee' boat from Guadalcanal back to Tulagi. The little cargo craft was in fact a tuna fishing boat that had been pressed into service out of San Diego and was now doing a vital shuttle and supply service between Guadalcanal and Tulagi. The PTs were ordered to see the little craft safely into Tulagi, and by the time they arrived that evening it was too late to do anything about the Japanese delivering a bombardment of over 760 eight-inch shells which served as a cover for fresh Japanese reinforcement landings near Tassafaronga. The morning of 15 October revealed a disheartening sight. Enemy transports standing off the point calmly unloaded troops and supplies while aircraft and destroyers hovered over and around them as a screen. Japanese commanders were confident that the night's bombardment had silenced Henderson Field's planes, but they were wrong. Through Herculean efforts, Marine planes were soon in the air, fending off the Zekes to inflict heavy damage on the landing forces. Several of the transports were run aground and abandoned on the beach, and shortly the Japanese turned tail and headed for home. Even then the situation on Guadalcanal was critical. The following night cruisers *Myoko* and *Maya*, escorted by Tanaka's destroyers, once again pounded Henderson Field and nothing – including the PT-Boats at Tulagi – could sortie to meet

Three 77-footers head out for an evening patrol. Once out of the harbor, boats would separate into groups of two and head for their assigned sectors where, theoretically, anything that moved was fair game.

Center Left
PT-115 was one of the first Elco 80-footers to meet the enemy when, as one of the elements of Squadron 6, she went into action in some of the later duels with the 'Tokyo Express' off Guadalcanal. The 115 is seen here cruising Tulagi Harbor during July 1943. By this time the Japanese had given up Guadalcanal, and the heavy fighting was moving west into the vicinity of other squadrons. Note that while it would still be some time before the torpedo tubes were replaced with launching racks for the Mark XIII, this boat has already received its field-installed radar, the original mast having been removed in favor of a heavier type supporting the radar dome containing the sweeper antenna. In 1944 this type of radar began to be phased out with the introduction of an even more advanced version. This boat survived the war only to be disposed of at the end of hostilities by burning. The fact that at this time PTs were still primarily concerned with ship hunting is evidenced by the lack of secondary armament: the boat carries only the standard weaponry installed at the factory. Later a 40 mm and additional 20 mm and 37 mm guns would be added.

Bottom Left
At the entrance to Tulagi Harbor lie two tiny jungle-covered pieces of land dubbed the 'Sing Song Islands' by the PT sailors. According to Bob Searles, the islands were so named because the native name for the islands 'sounded something like that'. The islands were landmarks for boats returning from combat at morning's first light.

Top Right
An Elco 77-footer running at top speed. Those crewmen who operated these boats during the early battles off Guadalcanal generally liked their mounts better than the 80-footers which began to arrive a few months later, this mainly because they felt the 77-footer was a more nimble craft. It was clearly understood that such a factor could be of importance when weaving in and out of a column of fast moving Japanese destroyers.

Bottom Right
An Elco 80-footer cruises off the Tulagi shoreline during early 1943. The apparently serene tropical setting was not only infested with Japanese, but with all manner of additional health hazards including disease and poisonous insects and animals.

Right
Hugh Robinson, commander of Squadron 3 (right) and Lt Lester Gamble, the squadron's leading ace as far as torpedo hits on enemy ships were concerned, are seen in this early 1943 photograph while on leave shortly after the heavy fighting off Guadalcanal had come to a close.

Bottom
A group of Tulagi-based PTs including both 77-footers of Squadron 3 and 80-footers of Squadron 6. An Elco 80-footer which appears to be PT-116 has had a shark's mouth painted on the bow by enterprising crewmen. This photograph would have been taken around the first few months of 1943.

A view from the pier at Tulagi showing a number of the base's PTs nosed into the shore. Note that one of the boats carries a very early experimental radar installation, the dome being visible on about the fifth boat in line.

them. Admiral Nimitz grimly conceded: 'It now appears that we are unable to control the sea in the Guadalcanal area. Thus our supply of the positions will only be done at great expense to us. The situation is not hopeless, but it is certainly critical.'

The last two weeks of October saw incredibly heavy ground fighting on Guadalcanal, the Japanese High Command having resolved to capture Henderson Field by the end of the month with the aid of 4,500 newly arrived troops. What they could not know was that Roosevelt had decided the United States could not afford to lose the lower Solomons and had resolved to reinforce the effort even at the expense of delaying other operations being carried out in a global war. But although this directive was handed down to the Joint Chief's of Staff on 24 October, it would be weeks before its effects were felt in any material sense. In the meantime the United States Navy and the Marines would have to hold out as best they could.

On 25 October the second division of Squadron 3 pulled into Tulagi, their crews looking forward to action, especially after listening to crewmen of the first four boats recounting the particulars of their initial encounter with the enemy. Every one of the men who would ride the PTs during the night missions to come now realized that knocking off Japanese ships with dashing impunity was something for prewar newspaper stories. Night games between modern warships and glorified cabin cruisers was going to be deadly business, but this realization seemed only to sharpen the resolve of these men in their determination to prove that their boats could make a valuable contribution to the war.

One thing that the PT-Boats did have on their side was an outstanding intelligence network spread out all up and down the Solomon Islands. From the moment the Japanese lit their boilers at their anchorage off Bougainville or any of the other island harbors used as staging areas, coastwatchers fed the information on down the line. Ships planning to make night resupply runs would have to start their journey the day before, and so snooping observation planes could keep tabs on the convoys at least until dark. The big problem was simply in catching the Japanese. Admiral Tanaka would bring his fast destroyers steaming down the Slot at 35 knots, reaching the entrances to Guadalcanal Sound, or Iron Bottom Bay as it was known forever after, well into the night. Typically, he would zip past the Japanese-held portion of Guadalcanal, dumping supplies over the side in steel drums which would then theoretically wash ashore with the tide. Tanaka and his column of eight or ten destroyers would barely have to slow down. These resupply efforts were not of great strategic importance – but the enemy was there and it did offer a chance to shoot at him. The trouble was that bringing American ships in to do battle with Tanaka also allowed him the chance to shoot back, as was painfully demonstrated at the end of November when a specially trained United States cruiser task force tried to intercept and derail the Tokyo Express and was cut to ribbons by Japanese torpedoes for their efforts. Torpedoes from the Japanese DDs sank, in a single night's action, the cruiser *Northampton*, and so damaged three additional heavy cruisers (*Minneapolis*, *New Orleans* and *Pensacola*) that none would be back in the war in less

than a year. Since the turn of the century the Japanese Navy had put great thought and effort into developing destroyers, torpedoes and tactics, and while Japanese strategic thinking may have been faulty, their tactical procedures were, at least in the early years of the war, often very impressive.

To demonstrate how deadly it could be riding about the Pacific looking for Japanese destroyers in the dark, take for example a PT sortie on the night of 29–30 October. Coast-watchers reported ship movements in the form of three destroyers heading for Guadal-canal, doubtless intent upon a minor re-supply effort. Several of the Tulagi PTs got underway at nightfall, including PT-39 under Lt James Greene and PT-38 skippered by the now veteran (after one encounter with the enemy) Bob Searles. From the north Iron Bottom Sound is entered by either one of two narrow passages, one between Guadalcanal itself and the smallish Savo Island – which is the lower entrance – and one between Savo and Florida Islands. This upper entrance was the larger of the two, being about sixteen miles wide. After the initial action on 14 October, a little forethought made it quite clear that the target area of any Tokyo Express supply run was geographically quite limited and that the best possibility of

Two of the original combat veterans of the Tulagi-based PT-Boats of Squadron 3, Lts Hugh M. Robinson (left) and Jack Searles. Aboard one of the squadron's Elco 77-footers, which has had its cabin windows plated over to ensure that no light escapes from below during combat operations, the two officers display one of the boats' PT insignia. The insignia were normally affixed to either side of a boat's cabin, but were removed temporarily when the boats reached the combat area. It was realized that at a distance the bright white dots made perfect aiming points for enemy gunners. This insignia has been decorated with thirteen Japanese flags, one flag for each torpedo hit the squadron claimed. Shortly before this photograph was taken, Searles had relieved Robinson as squadron commander.

making contact with the enemy ships would be to station boats on either side of both passages and, if enough boats were available for duty on any one night, patrol the passages themselves. The chances of one boat making contact with the enemy were greatly increased, and when contact was established the other boats could be alerted to the location by radio. This strategy precluded any sort of massed attack, but single boats exercising great stealth now seemed to be the best means of getting close to an enemy while avoiding the very real possibility of a high-speed collision between the boats.

The 39 boat proceeded to its agreed patrol location outside the lower entrance to the sound to act as an advance scout along with PT-38, which would patrol a little to the north. With 30 October only a few minutes old, Greene radioed that he had sighted two ships off Cape Esperance heading northeast toward Savo Island. But the vessels were moving so fast that they soon disappeared into the darkness again. He was hoping that the 38 would heed his call, for it looked like a perfect setup. Knowing the enemy was on the way, Searles in PT-38 was still unable to make contact until it was almost too late, for the DD had apparently already spotted the PT when a friendly snooping spotter plane dropped a large flare over the speeding destroyer. Somehow it was now bearing down on the 38 from the east rather than from the south. Or was it a different destroyer that had slipped through into the bay undetected? While the destroyer opened up on the low-flying plane Searles gratefully jammed his throttles forward and headed in the general direction of home. Momentarily, the destroyer wheeled around and began lobbing shells at the fleeing PT. Searles broadcast a hasty radio message: 'One enemy can coming from east through Cape Esperance and Savo. Am being chased. Am being fired on. Course northeast. Hurry, Hurry!' The destroyer continued the chase for a few minutes and then abruptly broke away to the west through the lower passage, apparently intent upon going home. But Greene, having heard Searles' plea for help, was heading for the action when he picked up the retiring destroyer's wake. He turned to an overtaking course and at full speed soon found himself crawling up the stern of the enemy DD. Greene angled the 39 off to one side, turned back in toward the target and let go with three torpedoes. As he passed about two hundred yards astern of the vessel he thought one of his fish hit the destroyer amidships.

The record for this evening's action is inconclusive. There is no indication from postwar research that a destroyer was hit or sunk on 30 October, but Searles' experience with almost being run down serves to illustrate the hazard of serving aboard one of the early PTs. Later on, as the Allies advanced further up the Solomons, another PT skipper would have a similar encounter. Unfortunately for him, however, there would be no friendly spotter on hand to warn of the impending danger. A Japanese destroyer moving at better than 30 knots would cut an 80 ft Elco boat, PT-109, in half bringing injury and death to a crew led by Lt John Kennedy.

The action of 30 October also serves to illustrate to what great advantage these early PTs could have used radar. Radar installations in PT-Boats was not far off, but by that time most of the big ship targets would be gone (or were out of reach for the PTs), and the new electronics would be used primarily for pinpointing barges to be gunned down. Interestingly enough, as a comment on the general theory of using fast torpedo boats to sneak up on unsuspecting warships under the cover of darkness, the wholesale introduction of radar into warships would spell the end of the concept of torpedo boats. With reliable radar, ships could easily locate approaching torpedo boats long before they reached torpedo range and in plenty of time to fend off the torpedo boats with gunfire.

*   *   *   *   *   *

During the first nights of November 1942 the Japanese continually ran the Tokyo Express in and out of Guadalcanal, the decks of their destroyers – and even an occasional cruiser – were loaded with men and supplies which would be lightered off by small boats in the night. PTs were ordered to patrol on these nights but had little to show for their efforts. Stilly Taylor in PT-39 and a Japanese destroyer surprised each other on the night of 4–5 November, the destroyer opening up with all guns and driving the 39 off before Taylor could maneuver for a shot.

The Tulagi PT force had better luck the following night when, in the early hours of 6 November, Lt Les Gamble, snooping about in PT-48, managed to creep to within four hundred yards of a destroyer without being spotted. At this close range Gamble gave the order to fire all four tubes and was rewarded with two tremendous explosions amidships of the Japanese DD. As PT-48 turned a few rounds of shell-fire flew harmlessly overhead. Had the 48 sunk a ship? Again, it would never be confirmed. Patrolling aircraft spotted an oil slick and wreckage floating about the next morning, but postwar investigation was inconclusive. Such were the rewards for the PT sailors.

Two nights later the PT forces were called upon again. Intelligence reports indicated a force of five destroyers heading down the Slot from Bougainville, and all available PTs were ordered to intercept. Of the eight boats in the squadron at this time only three were able to nose out of the harbor that night. As Lt Savage, squadron intelligence officer, noted in his log book that day:

'This was the third time in four nights that the PT-Boats had been out to clash with a strong enemy force. With the inadequacy of base facilities and the constant use of the boats, proper maintenance had become a problem. The boat's own officers and men, after spending a nerve-shattering night battling heavy Jap ships that repeatedly caught them in blinding lights and on occasions all but blew them out of the water with deadly salvos of explosive shells, would catch a few hours nap in the early morning, then spend the major portion of the day working to have the boats in shape for the night's patrol. Morale was high, but physical strain was beginning to show in men and boats.'

One of the squadron's ace skippers, Lt Les Gamble, commented on the subject of fatigue: 'You knew you had to stay alert to stay alive out on patrol. But you would get so tired that you would actually go to sleep on your feet. I don't know whether I was dreaming or halucinating, but I remember looking up one night and seeing a golden aircraft-carrier being pulled across the sky by sixteen golden horses. On another occasion I was driving the boat after a long patrol, and suddenly there was a giant brick wall right in front of me. Luckily, I woke up before we hit the wall.'

Squadron Commander Hugh M. Robinson, who had replaced the physically debilitated Montgomery upon his arrival with the second four boats in late October, led his three-boat force out into the night. Aboard PT-61, Robinson was accompanied by Greene in the 39 boat and Lt Leonard Nikoloric in PT-37. The three boats intercepted a column of enemy destroyers south of Savo Island and fanned out to attack. PTs 37 and 39 were both able to draw beads on targets and each got off two torpedoes. As the 27 knot fish approached their victims, the destroyers turned into the attack to present the smallest possible target with the result that all four torpedoes missed. Now it was the enemy's turn to make life uncomfortable for the mosquito boats. Searchlights blazed into the darkness and picked up the now fleeing PTs. Very heavy fire soon followed. Robinson aboard the 61 vividly recalled the action:

'We had turned away from the destroyers

Left

These two views show an 80 ft Elco boat that would later become the most famous of all PTs to participate in World War Two. PT-109, the boat which would have as its last skipper a Lt John F. Kennedy, is seen here lashed to the deck of a cargo ship during August 1942. The two photos were taken for the specific purpose of showing the proper way to stow a PT-Boat aboard a cargo ship, the photographer undoubtedly oblivious of the number carried by the boat he happened to choose as his subject. At this time the 109, as part of Squadron 5, was being shipped to the Panama Canal for duty in that area. Once there the boat would be transferred to Squadron 2 just before that group's shipment to Tulagi in the Solomons. Squadron 2 would join Squadron 3 in late 1942 to do battle with the 'Tokyo Express'. The 109 would survive several meetings with Japanese destroyers while based at Tulagi, meeting her end after moving up in the Solomons to a new base at Rendova.

Right

PT-107, torpedo tubes cranked out into the firing position, rigs up for a tow from an escorting tender. The boat is seen here en route to its new base at Rendova in the Solomons. This boat would have been in the same squadron as Jack Kennedy's PT-109, the two boats being virtually identical in arrangement.

and were making top speed trying to clear the area when a shell zipped right over the cockpit – it couldn't have cleared our heads by more than a few inches – and landed on the bow, blowing a large section of it away. I kept the throttles full forward, and by making top speed we managed to keep any water from shipping in. When we pulled into Tulagi harbor and I brought the boat down off its plane, we immediately started taking water in the hole.'

While these first nights of November were debilitating enough for both boats and men, they were as nothing compared to what was in store. By 9 November Allied intelligence experts sensed that something big was brewing. Air reconnaissance indicated a buildup of forces at several Japanese bases and it was surmised that a large amphibious operation supported by heavy warships would be undertaken very soon, possibly reaching Guadalcanal by 13 November. It was a race against time, for the first of the reinforcements committed by the Joint Chiefs as a result of the Presidential directive to hold Guadalcanal were also headed for the island. With luck, 6,000 men and thousands of tons of supplies and equipment could finish going ashore one day before the Japanese arrived. With anything less than luck, this great effort could become a disaster. Fat transport ships unloading in broad daylight make excellent targets. In immediate support of the United States cargo ships were five cruisers and eight destroyers which would have to deal with any Japanese strike force. Further to the north was a task force consisting of the carrier *Enterprise* and two of the new fast battleships, *Washington* and *South Dakota*. But the man in command of this group, Rear Admiral Thomas C. Kinkaid, preferred to keep his ships as backup for the operation, allowing only the planes from the *Enterprise* to become involved in the battle area by virtue of their being able to use Henderson Field as a refueling stop.

The transports got out just in time. As they steamed away to safety, the escorting force, consisting of cruisers *San Francisco*, *Portland*, *Helena*, *Juneau* and *Atlanta* as well as eight escorting destroyers, doubled back to meet a reported enemy force heading down the Slot. Supplies were still scattered all about the beach on Guadalcanal, and if the Japanese were allowed to shell the Marines as usual, the results would almost certainly be catastrophic. Under the command of Admiral Richmond K. Turner – who would lose his life in this battle – the Americans would turn back the far superior Japanese bombardment force of two battleships, one light cruiser and eight destroyers. In a wild half-hour battle the United States predictably lost one cruiser, the *Atlanta*, and the destroyers *Barton*, *Laffey*, *Monssen* and *Cushing*, and suffered damage to the other four cruisers as well. But the Japanese also suffered. The battleship *Hiei* took over fifty hits and was finally sunk the next day by planes from Henderson Field. Those planes were able to take off because, although they had inflicted heavy damage on the Americans, the Japanese turned for home after the battle, failing to drop a single shell on the Marines on Guadalcanal. This opening engagement in the early hours of Friday 13 November 1942 marked the beginning of the great Naval Battle of Guadalcanal.

An Elco 80-footer is high and dry in a floating drydock while two more boats are tied up alongside. These floating drydocks were an essential part of PT operations as it was absolutely necessary for the boats to have their bottoms cleaned and wood dried out on a regular basis. This photo was taken at Funafuti in the Ellice Islands. There was virtually nothing for the few boats stationed here to do other than run daily security patrols. It was, however, a group of boats based at Funafuti that rescued Captain Eddie Rickenbacker after he and his party had spent days at sea in a life-raft following the crash of their plane.

On the night of 13–14 November everyone on Guadalcanal knew what was coming, and there was no one around to stop it – or almost no one. The Japanese steamed into the sound with two heavy cruisers and a brace of escorting destroyers. The plan was for this group to plaster the Marines and troublesome Henderson Field so that Tanaka could bring a super Tokyo Express down the Slot the next day without interference from air attack. Ten fast troop transports escorted by eleven of Tanaka's destroyers would, the Japanese were confident, turn the tide on Guadalcanal. The battle for control of the lower Solomon Islands had reached a critical point for the Allied forces. The Japanese could not be allowed to put Henderson Field out of commission. As far as the United States Navy was concerned, on that particular night, there were only two things that could possibly stop the Japanese bombardment force. One was PT-38 and the other was PT-39.

That evening the two PTs had been assigned the task of screening the damaged cruiser *Portland* (hit the night before) while she was being towed back to Tulagi. The boats split up to enable them to patrol more territory. According to Stilly Taylor of the 39 boat:

'By about twelve-thirty we were secured from this job and immediately tried to locate each other again. However, before we were able to do so, the Nips began to shell Henderson Field, first putting a very bright flare in the vicinity of the field, and naturally both of us started in on them independently.

'Apparently I was much nearer to the Japs than Jack was (Jack Searles in PT-38) because of where I had secured from patrol around the *Portland*. The best intelligence we had was that there was a Jap battleship on the way down from either Bougainville or Rabaul. It was supposed to have been accompanied by several escorts, probably destroyers.

'As soon as the Japs opened fire, it was obvious to us that there was at least one fairly heavy ship. We thought, at the time, that it was probably the battleship referred to in the intelligence report. We could tell that it was definitely a heavy ship because of the long orange flash from its gunfire rather than the short white flash which we knew from experience was the smaller fire of the destroyers. As we started in to make our run on this formation, we thought that we saw a destroyer make a short scouting trip well ahead of the main formation. My quartermaster reported this, and I could never be

While traveling from Torokina, Bougainville to Treasury Island as an escort for an LCT, PT-167, a zebra-striped Elco 80-footer, was attacked by a dozen Japanese torpedo bombers that tried everything short of crashing on the tiny convoy to score a hit. Indeed, as the 167's gunners pumped shells into a torpedo plane that passed so low overhead it took away the PT's mast, the crew felt a heavy jolt but did not have time to investigate the source at the moment. After the planes withdrew, an unseen torpedo was discovered to have porpoised through the bow without exploding.

absolutely sure that it was not his imagination. However, due to the light put up by the Nips' flares, I was able to use my [torpedo] director for the first time. I set his speed at about 20 knots and I think that he was doing slightly more than this. I kept him in the director for approximately seven salvos, and really had a beautiful line on him.'

PT-39 continued to bore in on the heavy ship until the range closed to about 1,000 yards. Taylor felt that if he closed any further he would be discovered by the destroyer screen that he knew must be protecting the bigger ships. He gave the order to fire all four torpedoes. Three hit the water beautifully, but the fourth misfired and never left the steel tube. The 39 wheeled hard around and headed for home, its night's work done no

matter what the result. Skipper Taylor later reported, 'I am positive that at least one of them found its mark.'

Searles, coming in behind PT-39, also found a target. A Japanese destroyer, no doubt one of the screening group for the cruisers, crossed the path of the 38 and Searles let go with a full spread. His crew claimed they saw two of the fish strike home.

'This was an easy attack for PTs because', according to Taylor, 'we were able to get within range unmolested with good visibility because of their flares and because of their gunfire. I do believe that the first they knew of our presence was when torpedoes hit them. It was the kind of attack that we had all been dreaming about. They usually came in under cover of bad weather, and we often found ourselves in the middle of them before we knew what was going on'.

Typically, results of this action are unconfirmed. What is vitally important is that at the mention of the word 'torpedo' Admiral Mikawa, in charge of the bombardment group, turned for home after destroying or damaging only about twenty aircraft on Henderson Field. A built-in horror of torpedoes might explain Mikawa's actions, whether he was hit or not. The Japanese were fully aware of how efficient and destructive

their own 'long lance' torpedoes were and might well have assumed that their American counterparts were nearly as dangerous. Such was not the case, for the American Mark VIII was an inferior relic from World War One. But the Japanese could not have known this at the time.

The next morning, planes based at Henderson or flying out of Henderson from the carrier *Enterprise* managed to sink six of Tanaka's troop-laden transports in a route that was truly the turning-point at Guadalcanal.

The very next evening, the PTs prepared for sea once again with the news that yet more Japanese warships would be in Iron Bottom Bay that night. According to Robinson, 'We got the word that more transports, destroyers and battleships would be coming in from the North West and that cruisers would be running through the passage south of Savo. We were ordered to go out to the west of Savo and seek targets of opportunity. They told us there was a possibility that Admiral Lee would be coming in from the South with a battleship force, but the feeling was that he would not arrive in time.'

Luckily for the PT sailors, heavy reinforcements were on the way in the form of the two new battleships, *Washington* and *South*

Another view of PT-169, taken at the same time as the picture opposite, is noteworthy in that on close examination it will be noticed that the port rear torpedo is in fact an old Mark VIII mounted in a Mark XIII launching rack (note that the port rear torpedo is much longer than the starboard rear Mark XIII). This is just one more example of the belief by the field forces that the old torpedoes could be launched from something other than a tube.

Dakota, which Admiral Halsey had finally-released from carrier screening duties so that Admiral Willis Lee could 'bust into Iron Bottom Sound and clean up', as Halsey put it.

Only three boats were serviceable that night. Robinson, Green and Nikoloric boarded their aging torpedo boats that evening and headed for Savo Island. Squadron Commander Robinson later recounted events:

'About halfway between Tulagi and Savo I heard a voice come over the radio and say, "Peter Tare, Peter Tare . . . this is Lee . . . Ching Lee . . . Ching Lee. Catchy?" I got on the radio and said, "Ching Lee, I understand". A voice came back, "Peter Tare . . . Peter Tare . . . stand clear . . . we are coming through". I turned my boat around and headed for home.'

There was little doubt among those who heard the transmission that the man on the other end was indeed the battleship task force commander. Everyone knew that Willis Lee had done a stretch on China Station before the war and had since often been referred to as Ching Chong China Lee. Contrary to popular versions of the event, the boats saw no ships before the radio message was received, and Lee had not seen any torpedo boats.

Robinson and Green took their boats back into Tulagi, tied up at the dock and then ran up to the top of a 500-foot-high hill at the back of the camp to watch the show. Nickoloric also withdrew off to the North East but did not go back into Tulagi immediately. According to the young PT skipper:

'We stopped our engines. Porterfield went below and made some sandwiches and coffee. We all went up and sat on the foredeck, and half an hour later we were all sitting there eating tuna fish sandwiches, sipping coffee and watching from a front-row seat one of the greatest battles of the war. It was like sitting at Ebbets Field.'

From his vantage point back atop the hill at Tulagi, Robinson recalled the night's action: 'It was a fantastic view. You couldn't really tell who was who but we assumed the two big ships off to the south were Lee's battle-wagons. It was a very clear night for a change with a bright moon shining. You could actually see the ships out in the bay. You would see the big guns fire and the shells go arching up into the sky in a bright red streak. And then they would start down and finally hit and blow the side completely out of some ship. There wasn't much in the way of cheering – we were all mostly awestruck by the spectacle.'

After this climactic three-day struggle, ending with Lee's victorious charge into Iron Bottom Bay, the tempo of operations for the PT-Boats died down somewhat. This gave the Tulagi force time to do some much needed overhauling on their boats to improve combat availability. The situation was further helped by the arrival of Squadron 2 near the end of November. In addition to six of the old 77 foot Elcos, the squadron was equipped with six of the new 80-footers, the first of these boats to enter the combat area.

PT sailors were typically very jealous of their high-performance equipment and took a great deal of pride in their individual boats. Squadron Commander Robinson was later asked if the men aboard the older 77 foot boats were envious of the new 80-footers:

'There was no envy at all. In fact the men of Squadron 3 felt the 77-footers were better suited to the task at hand. With their more shallow V-bottoms, they were faster than the new 80-footers and were also more maneuverable. We felt that the new boats were really a compromise. They were a more comfortable boat, but that didn't mean a great deal when a Japanese destroyer was on your tail.'

The first week of December was reasonably quiet, but on the 7th, exactly one year after the bombing of Pearl Harbor, aerial reconnaissance indicated nine destroyers were headed down the Slot. The Tokyo Express was back in business again and bent on another resupply effort for the now starving Japanese troops on Guadalcanal. The area commander now had the luxury of being able to send out eight PT-Boats to meet the enemy including PTs 36, 37, 40, 43, 44, 59 and 109. PT-109, skippered by Squadron

PT-169 is seen during January 1944 returning to its base at Green Island during the morning after a patrol. While still equipped with the old 21 in torpedo tubes and Mark VIII torpedoes, this boat was in line behind PT-109 on the night the 109 was lost. The 169 fired two torpedoes at the destroyer *Amagiri* after it had rammed the 109, but the range was less than 150 yards and Lt Philip Potter, skipper of the 169, felt that his torpedoes probably hit the destroyer but did not have time to arm. As seen here, the boat has been equipped with a 37 mm gun on the bow for barge busting. Note the movie camera set up on the bow just ahead of the cabin.

Commander Rollin Westholm, was one of the new 80-foot Elcos, and all hands were anxious to see how the new boat would work out in combat.

The night's action opened when veterans Stilly Taylor and Bob Searles in PTs 40 and 48 spotted the destroyer column bearing down on them from their positions off the northwest tip of Guadalcanal. As the two boats swung out to get into firing position, two of the 48's engines inexplicably died. It was the worst possible moment for such an occurrence. Slowed to a crawl, the 48 was spotted and taken under fire by the DDs. Taylor, determined to do what he could for his old friend, opened his throttles and cut between the 48 and the onrushing destroyers, laying a smoke screen as he went. The sucker play worked, for the enemy turned to follow PT-40. Within minutes, Taylor had shaken off the pursuers, having given Searles time to idle off to safety.

PTs 40 and 48 were intended to act as scouts while four of the boats lay in wait near Savo Island. When word came over the radio from the 40 and 48 as to the enemy's heading, PTs 37, 36, 44 and 59 moved out into the passage to make their intercept. As the four PTs spotted the enemy column they deployed for attack and likewise came under immediate fire. One by one the boats unleashed their fish, the 37 leading the attack with two shots at the first destroyer. Right behind came battle-weary PT-59 which also dropped two silver missiles into the water. As the 59 wheeled around in her getaway she passed within 300 feet of her target, insanely close to such a heavily armed warship. Automatic weapons fire ripped through the wooden hull, but the game PT fought back, raking the DD's superstructure with hundreds of .50 caliber hits from her four machine-guns. Unfortunately all the torpedoes either missed or failed to explode.

As the 59 cleared the area, in came PTs 44 and 36, both boats emptying their tubes at the onrushing enemy. Both boats then turned and fled, not staying on hand long enough to observe any results. But in the middle of the attack, Westholm in PT-109 – which had been deployed a few miles to the east further into the sound – came roaring in to see if he could get in on the action. As he approached, his crew heard a violent explosion at about the time, it was learned later, the eight torpedoes fired by 44 and 36 would have arrived at their destination. The only conclusive result from this action was perhaps the most important. Whoever was in command of those five Japanese ships ordered an about-face and headed for home to arrive in the shelter of their harbor the next day – their

decks still full with men and supplies. One has to wonder how many Marines would live as a result of a few hundred fresh troops failing to reach the Japanese positions on Guadalcanal.

By now sixty days of continuous activity was starting to show among the personnel who had been the first to arrive back in October. Meeting the enemy night after night and then working all day long to keep the tired boats in commission was having its effect. Stilly Taylor later commented on the condition of the men:

'Our effectiveness fell off 100 per cent. We had had enough; we were no good any more. All of us had malaria or dengue fever or dysentery. We had all lost between ten and thirty pounds and were terribly nervous. We weren't closing properly with the enemy any more. Everytime we reported in before a patrol we would be wringing with sweat. We prayed that the Japs wouldn't come down. We were no good anymore. About the only thing that held us together was (Squadron Commander) Robbie Robinson's leadership and understanding.'

Like other portions of this account by some of the original squadron officers, this hindsight view may suffer somewhat from overstatement, for on the night of 9 December Jack Searles and his crew displayed a bit of the aggressiveness and quick thinking for which they had been chosen originally. Earlier in the day a message had been received at Tulagi to the effect that an intercepted and decoded Japanese communiqué indicated that a submarine would surface close to shore the next morning, at about 2.00 am, to deliver some high-ranking personnel. The message suggested that a volunteer force of PT-Boats attempt an intercept.

By the appointed hour, Jack Searles in PT-59 and Frank Freeland in PT-44 were on hand poking around a short distance off the Japanese-held portion of the Guadalcanal coast hoping to give a Japanese submarine a surprise reception.

At about the expected time the two boats spotted the submarine lying to on the surface. The two PTs were separated by about 500 yards, and the sub had popped up right between them. Freeland was not in firing position, but Jack Searles was. He launched two torpedoes at very close range, and the submarine disappeared in a violent explosion. Investigation confirmed the sinking of the 320 ft I-3 with a heavy loss of life. It was a long shot that paid off for the PT sailors and was a big boost for morale at the base. Later, discussing the mission, Searles remarked to Freeland that he could not under-

stand what had happened to the second torpedo as it could hardly have missed at such close range. Freeland replied that the second fish must have passed under the submarine, for he had seen its track go wizzing under his boat soon after the first explosion. Searles almost bagged two targets that night!

Two nights later on 11 December, the wooden wonders from Tulagi met the enemy again, this time in the form of another Admiral Tanaka special. With the word that the Tokyo Express would be running, five boats were made ready for patrol. Les Gamble in PT-37, Stilly Taylor in PT-40 and executive Bill Kreiner in Bob Searles' PT-48 were to proceed to Savo Island where they could lie in hiding under the southeast side of the island just offshore, hoping to catch Tanaka as he slipped through the passage between Savo and Guadalcanal's northern tip, Cape Esperance. Kreiner was by now an experienced veteran, and it was not unusual to allow an executive officer to take one of the boats out on patrol in the skipper's absence. In this case Bob Searles had been sent to Guadalcanal for a few days with the assignment of acting as liaison between the PT forces and any other elements that might be active in their patrol areas. Primarily it was his job to inform Marine aviators flying night missions where the PTs would be patrolling on any given night, so as to avoid unfortunate accidents due to mistaken identity.

The other two boats of the attacking force that night would be PT-44, commanded by Frank Freeland and Charlie Tilden in PT-110 – an Elco 80-footer. They were assigned what had come to be known as the 'bitch patrol' in the choppy waters off Kamimbo Bay at the western end of Guadalcanal.

By midnight the three boats off Savo were in position. They did not have long to wait. Unlike most nights when the Express ran, the evening was relatively clear. The three boats had lost visual contact with each other but all three soon spotted what appeared to be at least five enemy destroyers proceeding in column down through the Slot. Radios crackled, and the boats began to idle out into the passage at about 10 knots, trying to work themselves into firing position. Within moments of each other, each boat fired a spread of torpedoes, and then turned to scoot back into the protective lee of Savo. As they snuck away, one of the destroyers erupted with two massive explosions. The brand-new destroyer *Terutsuki* was mortally hit, and none other than Admiral Tanaka himself, whose flag the new ship carried, was injured in the blast. This was more than even Tanaka could take. He ordered another of his destroyers alongside the burning *Terutsuki*, transferred

An excellent view of one of the first production
Elco 80-footers, PT-107, running with sister boat
PT-108, in the background, during Squadron 5's
period of deployment to the Panama Canal.
Squadron 5 would be sent to the Solomon Islands,
but not until the spring of 1943, several months
after the initial bitter fighting and naval actions
off Guadalcanal involving the boats based at
Tulagi. Squadron 5's first base where they could
meet the enemy would be Rendova. During the
final phase of operations in the Solomons, while
based at Homestead Lagoon, Emirau Island, PT-
107 would meet its accidental end in a gas dock
fire on 18 June 1944.

As an element of Squadron 10 based at Green
Island in the northern Solomons during January
1944, PT-174 was in on some heavy barge busting
activity. As a result crewmen mounted a field-
modified 40 mm gun on the bow of the boat, but
only after some substantial strengthening of the
deck frames. The 174 was one of the few boats to
carry such a weapon on its bow. Six months
before this photograph was taken the 174 had
launched four torpedoes at a Japanese destroyer –
and claimed the only hit of the evening – on the
same night and in the same area in which PT-109
was cut in half.

During March 1944 two PTs of Squadron 10 are
seen nosed into a sandy beach on Green Island in
the northern Solomons. Gunner's mates load
drums of 20 mm aboard in preparation for a
night patrol. The tent arrangement on the bow of
the 168 was common practice in the tropics.

his flag and headed for home – his resupply mission thoroughly frustrated. But as it turned out, what Taylor and Gamble had figured to be a force of five destroyers actually numbered eleven, several of which stayed to patrol the sea. While the three boats lying off Savo had pulled off the perfect MTB attack, others would not be so lucky. Death would ride with the PTs this night.

As *Terutsuki* was being torpedoed, the two other PT-Boats patrolling the waters off the western end of Guadalcanal, PT-44 and PT-110, heard the radio chatter from the three boats lying off Savo and decided to turn around and head for Iron Bottom Bay, as that was where the action seemed to be this night. As the two boats entered the passage they passed fairly close astern of the burning destroyer, which gave cause for alarm to one of the officers aboard the 44. Just as Lt Chuck Melhorn mentioned to skipper Freeland that the fire from the burning destroyer might provide a perfect silhouette of the two fast-moving PTs for some other lurking enemy vessel, one of the enlisted men on the bridge spotted what Melhorn was most afraid of. Luckily the DD had not spotted the two boats, and Freeland swung the 44 around to begin lining up the destroyer for an attack. Just as this was done, however, two more

destroyers were sighted. To avoid being pinned between the two destroyers and the island, Freeland again changed course, this time to line up on the two new targets. But as the PT bore in, yet another destroyer spotted her against the burning *Terutsuki* and opened fire. The 44 swung hard around and began laying smoke as she headed for Savo Island to hide in the shadows if possible. Just south of Savo, Freeland turned the boat 180° to attempt another run on the destroyers. But as the boat came out of the turn she was fired upon by a destroyer that appeared out of the blackness a few thousand yards to the south. A single 4.7 in. shell hit the PT in the engine room, blowing a vast hole in the deck and setting the 44 on fire. Dead in the water now, she made a perfect target. The order was given to abandon ship, and as the first few men dove over the side the destroyer fired again, blowing the PT to splinters. Only two men survived this incident – one of the crewmen and Melhorn, who swam all the way to Savo Island and was picked up the next day.

*   *   *   *   *   *

Some weeks passed before the Tokyo Express ran again, thanks in no small degree

The vast reaches of the Pacific ocean set the stage for a 90° change of course to starboard for nine Elco 80-footers. This was occasionally used as an attacking maneuver, although boats on patrol at night were usually further apart.

to the rude reception Tanaka received on 11 December. After a month of recovery, Tanaka was ready once again for a resupply effort. He ran on 2 January 1942 and was attacked, Les Gamble claiming a hit. Patrols continued on a nightly basis, crews often rotating between operational boats to provide as many of the men as possible one day's rest for every mission they ran. When intelligence gave no indication of Tokyo Express activity, the boats would patrol close in off the Guadalcanal shore looking for barge traffic and submarines.

On the evening of 10 January four PTs had been sent out to patrol west of the passage between Savo Island and Cape Esperance on the tip of Guadalcanal. It had long since been learned that for routine patrols the most effective disposition of forces was to send the boats out in groups of two, each group assigned to patrol a particular sector of ocean. On this evening, Les Gamble in PT-45 and Lt Ralph Amsden, Jr in PT-39 patrolled the west side of the entrance to the passage while Bob Searles in the 48 and Ensign B.J.

Connolly in PT-115 covered the eastern side.

With the four boats already out on patrol, Squadron 2 leader Lt Westholm received word that eight Japanese destroyers would be arriving in Iron Bottom Bay about midnight. Such an opportunity called for a maximum effort on the part of the PT-Boat forces, and Westholm immediately ordered six additional boats to prepare to get underway. The squadron commander would skipper PT-112, which would be joined in a three-boat strike force by Lt Charlie Tilden in PT-43 and Lt Clark Faulkner in PT-40. These three boats would head for a sector immediately off the Guadalcanal coast just south of Cape Esperance, a very likely place for the destroyers to be making their drum-dropping runs. Westholm sent the other three boats – PTs 36, 46 and 59 – to patrol area a little further down the coast.

Apparently the Japanese ships managed to slip by the four boats guarding the entrance to the passage between Savo and Guadalcanal, because the first contact of the evening was made by Westholm. His three boats were idling slowly along about 400 yards offshore in an easterly direction, with Charlie Tilden's PT-43 in the lead. He was followed by Faulkner, with Westholm bringing up the rear. Suddenly Westholm spotted four destroyers even with their position and heading in the same direction – but about 1,200 yards further out. With the PTs hidden against the black background of the island it was the perfect setup. The Japanese ashore had lit small signal fires, apparently as a guide for the destroyers, but they were of no significance as far as silhouetting the PTs was concerned.

The squadron commander tried immediately to order the other two boats in for the attack, but was prevented from doing so thanks to a 'Black Cat' (Catalina flying boat patrol bomber) flying overhead whose pilot – on the same radio frequency as the PTs – was incessantly demanding to know, according to Westholm, 'What's going on down there? What's happening?'

Anxious moments passed, and finally Westholm was able to give the order to Tilden and Faulkner. Tilden, furthest to the east, turned the 43 out toward the enemy column and lined up on the leading destroyer. At the same time Clark Faulkner in PT-40 took careful aim at the second destroyer. Westholm, furthest west, pointed the nose of the 112 for the third DD in the column, the fourth ship having veered suddenly away out to sea for some unknown reason.

The three PTs each drew to within four to five hundred yards of their respective targets unobserved. The 43 was the first to launch, Charlie Tilden hitting the firing buttons for the aft two fish only to have the port tube produce a brilliant red flash as the torpedo made its exit. This was due, no doubt, to the black powder charge igniting grease and oil in the tube. Unfortunately for PT-43 this provided a perfect aiming point for the Japanese gunners aboard the destroyer. At 400 yards PT-43's torpedoes had somehow missed or failed to explode. It was clearly not Charlie Tilden's night and it was rapidly getting worse. He spun the wheel, putting the boat into a hard right turn, and then opened the throttles; but it was too late. The first Japanese salvo of 4.7 in. fire was close, the second right on target. The explosion ripped the PT, and as Tilden regained his footing he ordered the ship abandoned. The destroyer closed the stricken PT, spraying the water with machine-gun fire and passing so close that the survivors bobbing about in the water could hear the Japanese chattering on deck.

As Tilden's tube flashed, Faulkner in the center of the PT formation was also within firing range. Not taking any chances with this golden opportunity, he fired all four torpedoes at the second destroyer, dropped his exhaust baffles and opened the throttle wide, at the same time throwing the 40 into a hard right turn. As the PT gained speed, he watched one of his torpedoes strike the destroyer solidly, throwing a column of water high into the air. A secondary explosion followed an instant later. Faulkner angled PT-40 in close to the shore line, defying reefs and rocks as he ran flat out, heading southeast down the Guadalcanal coast. He knew that any pursuing destroyer could not follow, but there was a serious risk that his boat could be gutted at any second by an unseen rock just below the surface. Faulkner's luck held.

Meanwhile Westholm in the 112 had also launched a full spread of torpedoes at the last ship in line, one of which appeared to hit home, sending a geyser of water into the night sky. Knowing that this was the last ship in line, Westholm elected not to turn away, but to run ahead, shooting past his target's stern where he would then be free to streak for home. But there were now, unknown to the PT, other destroyers lurking further out and closing the scene of battle. Two ships off the port bow of the 112 opened fire, and within moments the tiny boat was hit in the bow and engine room by 4.7 in. shells. For some reason the destroyers did not close, and all hands had time to abandon ship via the life raft. The hulk of PT-112 was still afloat an hour later, so Westholm decided to paddle back to see if he could recover a pair of binoculars he particularly prized and had left on the bridge. As he drew to within about 100 feet, the 112 exploded and the question was settled.

With Stilly Taylor at the helm, PT-46 suddenly came roaring into the mêlée just as one of the Japanese destroyers had switched on its searchlight to illuminate PT-43, which, unmanned, had continued to make slow headway until it ran up on the Guadalcanal beach. Taylor lined up a target and fired a full spread at 1,800 yards. Within minutes explosions were observed at the target's waterline. The crew of the 46 felt some degree of retribution had been gained in exchange for the lives of their shipmates, which they feared had fallen into Japanese hands ashore. Luckily, the surviving members of the two crews bobbing about offshore were soon rescued, but the loss of two boats was a hard blow. By dawn, Japanese troops were crawling all over the hulk of the beached 43. A New Zealand corvette, affectionately known as 'Smokey Joe' due to the voluminous black smoke the ship seemed to spew forth from its stack at all times while underway, was called upon the scene and blew the wrecked PT into small pieces with gunfire.

Results? The PT sailors claimed hits on three ships, but nothing conclusive would be learned of the action other than confirmation that on the night in question the destroyer *Hatsukaze* had been holed through by a dud torpedo. But the next morning the Tulagi PTs were out merrily machine-gunning the hundreds of barrels the Japanese destroyers had rolled overboard.

*   *   *   *   *   *

The last big PT operation of the Guadalcanal campaign took place on the evening of 1–2 February. Intelligence reports gave every indication that the Japanese were mounting a massive resupply effort in the form of a super Tokyo Express consisting of as many as twenty destroyers. Such an enemy thrust called for help on everyone's part, Henderson Field-based aircraft being the first to strike the enemy in the late afternoon as the destroyers steamed down the Slot. But even more evidence that something big was up came in the form of heavy air cover sent down from Bougainville and other Japanese airstrips. The Marine aviators held their own against the enemy aircraft but managed to disable only one of the transport destroyers. Had the aviators been sharp enough to notice, they would have seen that these fast-moving destroyers carried no supplies or troops on deck. But then, it would have been too much to expect anyone on the American side to surmise that the Japanese had finally thrown in the towel. They were going to abandon Guadalcanal, and the fast transports were being sent down to pull off a well planned evacuation.

American destroyers – three *Fletcher*-class ships – steamed west to close with the enemy but were so hampered by concentrated air attacks that they were never able to reach the Japanese ships. Perhaps it was just as well, for three against twenty were poor odds and when destroyers met destroyers it usually resulted in a torpedo duel. In such a case, with their superior 'Long Lance' torpedoes, the Japanese would have had an additional overwhelming advantage. But PT-Boats had little to fear from torpedoes, and it soon appeared clear that the only United States Navy elements in the immediate area capable of engaging the enemy task force were the wooden wonders of Tulagi.

The men who boarded their PT-Boats that evening were scared. They had all been scared before, but this was different. Destroyers were the deadliest adversaries of the PTs and a force of twenty of the sleek, fast *Fubuki*-class ships were, the men knew, more than their force could hope to deal with. They would be happy to come out of this encounter with their lives. Some of them would not.

Every PT-Boat that could get underway was to participate in the night's activities. Westholm and Tilden in PTs 109 and 36 took a sector about two miles north of Doma Reef. Faulkner and Lt Ralph Richards of the newly arrived Squadron 6 took PTs 124 and 123 to an area about three miles due south of Savo Island to lie in wait for the enemy. About one mile northeast of these two boats, old hands Bob Searles and Stilly Taylor took up station in PTs 47 and 39. Closer to the passage between Savo and Guadalcanal on the Savo side, Les Gamble and Lt John Clagett waited in PTs 48 and 111. The last group to deploy consisted of three boats including Jack Searles in PT-59, Ensign Bart Connolly in PT-115 and Ensign J.J. Kelly in PT-37. This group was sent to a sector right off Cape Esperance which would have placed them in a likely position to be the first to meet the enemy.

It was a bad night for the PTs. Clagett in the 111 managed to fire all of his torpedoes at a destroyer but could not stick around long enough to observe results. Within minutes, while trying to make good his escape, his speeding PT was hit by shellfire and exploded in a burning inferno of gasoline-soaked mahogany. The crew spent the remainder of the night in the water, holding up the wounded and beating off sharks. Rescue came after daylight, but not before two of the crew had died.

Ensign Kelly in PT-37 also managed to get off four torpedoes at a destroyer, but in retiring was hit by 4.7 in. shell which penetrated the PT's gas tank and instantly turned the speeding boat into a fireball. One motor machinist's mate, blown through the side of the hull, survived the explosion badly burned; all others perished. Ensign Richards' PT-123 suffered a fluke end on this violent night as well. While stalking a target the torpedo boat was surprised by a Japanese floatplane that had flown up the boat's wake, cutting its engine as it glided in for the kill. The pilot placed a bomb squarely on the fantail of the 123. Four men were killed in the incident, the rest of the crew having to abandon ship almost immediately as flames engulfed the boat.

On the plus side, Ensign Connolly in PT-115 managed to sneak to within 500 yards of a destroyer, at which point he fired two torpedoes. As the 115 retired at high speed Connolly thought he saw two hits on the Japanese ship, after which it took on a definite list. The 115 was almost immediately taken in chase by two destroyers, and just as the shellfire was beginning to find the mark the PT was able to duck into a sudden rain squall the equal of the finest smoke screen. By now literally surrounded by destroyers, Connolly was able to con his ship through the ring to make for the safety of Savo Island, where he beached the PT until dawn.

Fortune also smiled on Clark Faulkner in the 124. Although Richards had been hit with a bomb as the two boats closed a target together, Faulkner managed to press home his attack, launching three torpedoes at 1,000 yards. After what must have seemed an eternity, the crew on the bridge watched two violent explosions rip the Japanese destroyer *Makigumo*. Although postwar interviews with officers of the Japanese ships indicated they felt that the ship had struck a mine (indeed 300 had been planted by United States minelayers that same day), this seems unlikely. The destroyer had to be abandoned.

Stilly Taylor, Les Gamble, Jack Searles and his brother Bob all had very close calls this evening as well. All had at one point or another been virtually surrounded by Japanese destroyers, most of which seemed intent on providing a screen while only about five actually loaded evacuees. As Bob Searles later recalled, 'We'd heard about the fall of the Japanese headquarters at Kolumbona and how the Japs on Esperance were hopelessly pocketed. Yet here was this armada of enemy ships steaming down, and we didn't know why they were coming or what they hoped to accomplish, and everyone had the feeling that our part of the fighting was never

going to end. Night after night for the rest of our lives we'd be doing this all over again, until the men cracked and the boats fell completely to pieces.'

But it was over, or at least the worst of it. From February on the Japanese would be fighting a retiring action all the way up the Solomons chain while American forces leap-frogged from one island to another, often simply bypassing Japanese strongholds that, while not attacked directly, would still have to be contained. This job would fall largely to the PT-Boat forces as they became proficient barge-busters – the Japanese employing this type of waterborne transport for lack of anything better in which to transport troops and supplies from one island to another. From Tulagi the PTs would move their front line bases to such famous names as Rendova, Vella Lavella and Cape Torokina, Bougainville. And although the PTs would occasionally meet Japanese destroyers in the following months, never again would they be involved with Japanese capital ships in the kind of intense, consistent action experienced at Guadalcanal.

In the end, one would have to ask what had been the accomplishments of the PTs that sortied from the Tulagi base to meet the Tokyo Express again and again for over four months. Perhaps squadron commander Hugh Robinson put it best when he said:

'We probably claimed more torpedo hits than we got – we found out later that many of our torpedoes were duds and that others would explode, for instance, in a destroyer's wake. But I think our major contribution to the campaign was that we posed a threat. Had we not been there, the Japanese would virtually have had their way at sea most of the time. They would have been free to supply their troops on the island, and whether or not this would have affected the final outcome of the battle isn't nearly as important as the number of American lives that were saved because the Japanese were too hungry or too tired or too ill-equipped to fight any longer than they did.'

The ace scorer of Squadron 3, Lt Les Gamble, summed it all up even more succinctly when he later commented, 'We were awfully glad when it was over.'

PT-105, the third production boat in the Elco 80-foot series, is seen here cruising off the Panama Canal as an element of Squadron 5 during early 1943. During the spring of that year, the squadron would be shipped to the Solomons and, although arriving too late to see any action off Guadalcanal, the boats in this group would do battle with the Japanese while operating out of Rendova, further north in the island chain. During late August 1943 PT-105 was one of several boats that participated in one of the first daylight PT raids in the Pacific. The idea was to strike at shore positions on Kolombangara on the 22nd of the month, this in the hope of catching the Japanese by surprise. Although provided with an air escort to fend off any patroling Zeros, the boats met with heavy fire from the shore and thereafter returned to their night fighting tactics.

PT-40, a battle-scarred veteran of the Guadalcanal campaign, is returned to Melville in July 1944 to be used as a repair training boat for new personnel.

6

Wild Nights in the Med

While their brethren in the Pacific challenged the mightiest of warships, the PT-Boats in the Mediterranean – for a time the only representatives of the U.S. Navy in that sea – came up against a different kind of enemy. Flak barges and E-Boats were potentially more deadly to PT-Boats than anything else they would try to tackle throughout the war.

September 1943 saw Allied armies invading the southern shores of the Italian mainland at Salerno immediately after conquering the large island of Sicily. At the same time the Italian armed forces surrendered – including the navy – but this meant not a great deal to the Allies as it would be the Germans who would tenaciously resist as the American and British Armies fought their way north up the Italian 'Boot' in the subsequent months.

By Spring 1944 the German attempt to halt the Allied thrust north was being seriously hampered through lack of supply. Although the Germans continued to put up heavy fighter resistance, they could not stop the onslaught of Allied fighters and bombers assigned the task of eliminating all transportation behind enemy lines. The railroad system was quickly destroyed, and truck convoys were so harassed by marauding fighter-bombers that they became ineffectual. Thus the Germans were forced into a scheme of supplying their forces in northern Italy by sea from their ports in southern France. This mainly took the form of cargo ships and other auxiliary craft travelling in small convoys down the coast at night.

A formidable system for the protection of these vital supply convoys was set up by the Germans all along their route. Minefields were laid out to sea forming a lane down which the shallow draft craft could travel, hugging the shore line, without worry of interdiction by British or American destroyers. The route was further protected by heavy batteries along the shore so that even if a heavy Allied warship were to dare the mines it would have to contend with guns lobbing shells as large as $9\frac{1}{2}$ in. in diameter. The convoys themselves almost always consisted in part of the heavily armed F-lighters, and

were often escorted by Flak lighters, S-Boats and even destroyers. The Germans had taken over from the Italian navy a number of small warships peculiar to that service that might best be described as a cross between a destroyer and a torpedo boat. Referred to by Allied commanders in their action reports as simply 'destroyers', these vessels were also used for convoy escort duty.

Captain J.F. Stevens, RN, Captain Coastal Forces, Mediterranean, commenting on operations during January and February 1944, said:

'There can be no question but that the interruption of the enemy's sea communications off the west coast of Italy presents a difficult problem. He has made extensive use of minefields to cover his shipping route, and while Coastal Forces are the most suitable forces to operate in mined areas, the enemy has so strengthened his escorts and armed his "shipping" that our coastal craft find themselves up against considerably heavier metal. Furthermore, the enemy's use of "F-lighters" of shallow draft does not provide good torpedo targets. Everything that can be done to improve our chances of successful attack is being done. Plans for diversionary attacks in the hope of breaking up an enemy convoy and cutting off stragglers have been made. Torpedoes will, if possible, be fired at even shallower settings. Meanwhile, if they cannot achieve destruction, Coastal Forces will harry the enemy and endeavour to cause him the utmost possible alarm, damage and casualties.'

As might be surmised from Captain Stevens' statement, the Allied Coastal Forces had come up against a problem that was proving difficult – and often costly – to deal with. The weaponry carried by the PT-Boats, and the

British MTBs (motor torpedo boats) with which they operated, was simply not heavy enough. During November of the preceding year, Lt-Commander Barnes' plan of a combined force – PT-Boats with their radar for scouting and coordination, MTBs with their superior torpedoes for protection against heavy enemy escort, and motor gunboats (MGBs) for engaging the transports with gunfire – was implemented. But the F-lighters had proved more than a match for even the MGBs.

The solution to this sticky problem was to come from the redoubtable Commander Robert Allan with the formation in March 1944 of the Coastal Forces Battle Squadron, the most spectacular and successful small boat unit of the war. By this time Allan was in operational command in the western area, with one flotilla each of MTBs and MGBs at his disposal along with Barnes' squadron of American PTs (Higgins) which would remain under British operational control throughout the entire Mediterranean campaign. From their base at Bastia on Corsica these boats could patrol the entire Gulf of Genoa. Allan's scheme was to build an attack force centered around three British LCGs (landing craft gun). Each of these craft mounted two 4.7 in. and two 40 mm guns, the 4.7 in. being manned by crack Royal Marine gun crews. The slower LCGs would, in turn, be screened from either destroyer or S-Boat attack by MTBs and MGBs while the American PT-boats again provided scouting and target information with their radar.

By 27 March the new attack force was assembled and prepared for its first operation. The battle line included LCGs 14, 19 and 20 escorted by MTB 634 and MGBs 662, 660 and 659. Scouting for the group would be PT-212 skippered by Lt. (jg) T. Lowry

Top

A fine study of PT-212, a 78 ft Higgins boat, as seen entering a floating drydock at La Maddalena off the north coast of Sardinia. This boat was one of the original members of Squadron 15 sent to the Mediterranean in April 1943 and which were for a time the only elements of the United States Navy in the area. This 1944 photo shows the boat after having had its original torpedo tubes replaced in favor of the Mark XIII launching racks. The 212 participated in a number of engagements with the enemy including 'Operation Gun' and, on several occasions, was among a group of boats which launched torpedoes against enemy ships with positive results. In October 1944 this boat was handed over to the British Coastal Forces on lend-lease. The boat appears to be painted in a Measure 31 paint scheme.

Bottom

One of the first boats of the United States Navy to operate in the Mediterranean, PT-211 was a member of Squadron 15. Pictured here during February 1944 tied up in Bastia Harbor, Corsica, this boat was eventually handed over to the British Coastal Forces in the area during October 1944.

Top Left

Seaman Michael Kalausky photographed this tranquil scene of the Bastia-based PTs nested within the town's seawall. Close examination will reveal that several of the boats are equipped with the Elco Thunderbolt quad 20 mm mount, while most of the PTs carry 40 mm cannon. In the background tied up just ahead of two Elco 80-footers is a smaller craft, an air/sea rescue or 'crash' boat. Further ahead by itself is a single gunboat. The crash boat is typical of the 55-footers built in some numbers during the war. They were equipped with only two Packard engines (and carried only two twin .50 caliber machine-gun turrets) but could make 55 knots, making them the fastest boats in service with the Navy. In the foreground are lined up six Elco 80-footers followed by three Higgins boats.

Bottom Left

During the Salerno Bay operations of September 1943, a zebra-striped Higgins boat stands guard offshore with part of the invasion convoy in the background. The effectiveness of the zebra paint scheme in confusing enemy gunners was at best questionable.

Top Right

A proud PT sailor poses in front of the cockpit of his Elco 80-footer, PT-559, while anchored in the harbor at Bastia. On the night of 14 June 1944 PT-559 was one of a three-boat force that located, tracked and attacked two German corvettes using radar bearings only. The 559 was also one of only four boats in the Mediterranean experimentally fitted with the Elco Thunderbolt quad 20 mm gun mount. The six kill marks on the bridge indicate participation in the sinking of six German vessels.

Center Right

Higgins PTs at Maddalena, Sardinia with a surrendered Italian corvette in the background. It was this type of ship – roughly equivalent to a destroyer escort – that so often engaged the Med-based PTs in mortal combat. Several of the type were sunk by PT torpedoes.

Bottom Right

An example of an MAS-boat, the Italian counterpart to the PTs in the Mediterranean. These 50 ft boats were designed for torpedo delivery only, the gunboat function being left to other types. The requirements of conducting operations in the relatively sheltered waters off the west coast of Italy and in the Aegean allowed the Italians to build and successfully operate considerably smaller torpedo boats.

117

Sinclair, USNR and PT-214 with Lt (jg) Robert T. Boebel, USNR, at the helm. These two Higgins boats were under the command of Lt Edwin A. DuBose, USNR, riding in PT-212. Their part of the mission was to search ahead of the main group and report target sightings. In the event of an engagement they had the additional responsibility of screening the main force from attack by the enemy destroyers that occasionally accompanied the lighter convoys. The last element of this miniature Allied task force was the control group consisting of PT-218 (Lt (jg) Thaddeus Grundy, USNR) and PT-208 (Lt (jg) John M. Torrance, USNR). Riding in PT-218 would be none other than Commander Robert A. Allan, RNVR, in command of the overall show. Besides providing tactical direction for the entire group, this control unit would also direct the fire of the LCGs by passing on bearings and ranges received on the PT's radar.

As the battle-line arrived off San Vincenzo early on the evening of the 27th DuBose's group was dispatched to make a fast sweep to the north in search of targets. At about 10 pm DuBose radioed back to Allan that they had located what was presumed to be six F-lighters heading south down the coast. With that, Allan moved his force quickly into position to make the interception. An hour later, as he lay waiting, Allan received another radio message from DuBose that the six F-lighters had a seaward escort of two destroyers which he would attack with torpedoes as soon as he could get his boats into position. Although within ten minutes Allan had picked up both the six F-lighters and the two screening destroyers on his radar screen, DuBose would have to do his work first. 'It was not possible', Allan recorded, 'for us to engage the convoy as our Starshells, being fired inshore over the target, would serve to illuminate us for the escorting destroyers which were to seaward. Fire was therefore held during many anxious minutes'.

What must have seemed like an eternity to Allan was actually about ten minutes, long enough for DuBose to bring his two PTs to within 400 yards of the two destroyers before being spotted and coming under heavy fire. Three torpedoes were launched, then the boats wheeled around and retired under smoke. As the throttles were opened, the 214 took a 37 mm shell hit in the engine room, damaging the center engine and wounding the Motor Machinist Mate. Through the smoke one of the destroyers was seen to spout a geyser but, typically, the extent of the damage could not be determined. What is important is that the two destroyers turned on their heels and headed north, abandoning

their charges to their fate.

Commander Allan wasted no time in ordering the LCGs to open fire. The first salvo of starshells lit the area beautifully and prompted the F-lighters to begin firing furiously into the air to repel an imagined air attack. The Royal Marine gunners aboard the LCGs needed no further opportunity. Within thirty seconds one of the F-lighters exploded with such force that even Allan was taken somewhat aback. A few minutes more, and three more of the lighters were ablaze. The two remaining F-lighters turned in an attempt to retreat from the battle but were pinned against the beach by the LCGs and pounded to very small pieces by 4.7 in. shells. 'Of the six (F-lighters) destroyed', Commander Allan reported, 'two, judging by the impressive explosions, were carrying petrol, two ammunition, and one a mixed cargo of both.' He then added almost wistfully, 'The sixth sank without exploding.'

'The outstanding feature of this operation', Allan went on, 'was the remarkable accuracy of the LCG's gunfire, but to enable this to function two most important factors cannot be overlooked. One was the excellent manner in which the LCGs carried out rather hurried manoeuvers. The other was the attack on the escorts by the Scouting PTs. This episode allowed the LCGs to fire undisturbed at the convoy and but for it this action might have developed very differently. It was, in fact, the crucial point of the whole engagement, and Lt E.A. DuBose, USNR, and Lt (jg) R.T. Boebel, USNR, are to be commended on their skill and courage in carrying out this attack. Also to be commended is Lt (jg) T. Grundy, USNR, who commanded the controlling PT with coolness and skill.'

Yet another spectacularly successful raid in what was known as 'Operation Gun' was brought off on the night of 24–25 April by Commander Allan's group, once again consisting of LCGs 14, 19 and 20 with Allan riding in PT-218 as the control unit, this time accompanied by PT-209. DuBose riding in PT-212 led the 202 and 213 boats as the scouting force and MTBs 640, 633 and 655 with MGBs 657, 660 and 662 rounded out the escort group tied directly to the LCGs. Again, it was the primary responsibility of this last group to fend off any possible attacks by 40-knot German S-Boats which the plodding LCGs could not hope to out-run.

As usual, the waters of the Tuscan Archipelago teemed with traffic after dark. The attack force left Bastia at different times owing to the respective speeds of the various component craft, but rendezvous was made off Vada Rocks at about 10 pm. Within five

minutes both the scouting and control groups had numerous radar contacts on their screens converging on the attack group from both the north and the south. Were both groups supply convoys – one fully loaded and heading south, the other empty and returning to Genoa or the French Riviera? Or could it be that the group approaching some twenty-five miles away from the south was a battle group intent on intercepting and escorting the lighters heading in from the north? Allan decided the most prudent course of action would be to wait and see. After considerable maneuvering to avoid contact until he chose to do so, Allan managed to remain undetected as the two enemy groups converged and passed each other. He then skilfully moved his LCGs into position for attack on the south-bound F-lighter convoy and, at 3,000 yards range, gave the order to his Royal Marine gunners to open fire.

Burning magnesium from the first star-shells revealed two F-lighters. Within three minutes both of the targets were vaporized in violent explosions as the LCGs' 4.7 in. shells struck home. Burning debris, thrown hundreds of feet into the night sky, set brush fires on the heavily wooded shore which, together with the fireworks from the exploding lighters, were visible as a brilliant display of lights some fifty miles away at the Bastia PT base on Corsica.

The remaining elements of the enemy were soon illuminated, their low silhouettes clearly discernible in the eerie green haze of the burning flares. Two F-lighters were immediately taken under fire and hit, along with a large oceangoing tug. The first lighter quickly disintegrated in a tremendous blast. The tug was quickly dispatched to the bottom as well. A second lighter burned furiously for a time, covering the entire area with a thick smoke cloud, and then was quickly gone in a large explosion. There was some doubt in Allan's mind as to whether additional targets had escaped by heading for the beach, so he dispatched his MGBs on a quick tour of the shoreline, while moving his battle group into position to intercept yet another radar contact coming down from the north. The MGBs found one beached F-lighter which they quickly set ablaze with gunfire, and managed to retrieve a dozen survivors.

As Allen gave the order to open fire on the new arrivals, three Flak-lighters were illuminated. Two of the craft never had a chance to return fire, luckily, for they were both hit on the first salvo from the three LCGs and were immediately cast in a grand fireworks display of exploding ammunition. But these escort lighters were not to be taken lightly, as was

Top

The most frequently encountered enemy vessel in the Mediterranean campaign was the German F-lighter. This was simply a diesel-powered shallow draft barge designed for hauling supplies and cargo. But when the British began to harass their supply convoys, the Germans took numbers of their F-lighters out of service and converted them to the infamous flak lighters. The flak lighter was simply an F-lighter that had been heavily armored and heavily armed with as many guns up to 88 mm in size as could be bolted in place. As a single hit from a German '88' could turn a PT-Boat into matchwood, attacking these craft was an extremely dangerous task even under the best conditions of surprise. This German flak lighter was photographed after the war at Ancona.

Bottom

Torpedoes were transported from United States factories in sealed steel tubes to prevent damage or corrosion to the complex and temperamental weapons. This scene is the torpedo storehouse at Palermo, Sicily.

Top
Beginning to show its age, the 80 ft Elco PT-559 passes through the Bastia seawall on its way out for a patrol. Note that this boat carries one of the Elco Thunderbolt guns covered over on the stern. Compare this photograph with earlier photos of Elco 80-footers equipped with torpedo tubes and it will become obvious that the introduction of the Mark XIII aircraft torpedoes provided marked savings in space and weight.

Top and Bottom Left
In the Mediterranean American PT-Boats operating in conjunction with British Coastal Forces often encountered their German counterparts, the famous *Schnellbooten* – (also known as E-Boats or S-Boats). A particularly well designed craft, these diesel-powered boats of 115 ft were constructed of aluminum frames and wooden planking and were actually capable of higher operational speeds than the American PTs. These boats were also particularly effective in the English Channel where they raided Allied shipping with telling effect during the first years of the war. The German torpedoes were, predictably, far more efficient than the early United States examples.

soon discovered when the third craft began to pour a tremendous volume of fire in the direction of the attack group. Shells of 20 mm, 40 mm and 88 mm rained about the LCGs, at which point Commander Allan ordered PT-218 to make a run on the Flak-lighter in order to draw its fire away from the slower LCGs. Before the PT-Boat could move in, the lighter took a serious hit and retired into the heavy smoke created by the first two victims of the Royal Marine gunners. The accompanying control boat, PT-209, was then ordered to pursue the damaged lighter and headed off into the smoke accompanied by several of the British MGBs. Charging through the night, the 209 soon spotted the enemy vessel. Lt Bill Eldredge at the helm ordered one torpedo fired, turned away and watched the enemy craft take a direct hit which split it in two.

For a while all was now quiet. To the north of the battle scene the three PTs of the scouting group had decided quietly to attempt to overtake the northbound enemy column which had been so carefully avoided earlier. Creeping to within firing range, the PTs launched a spread of torpedoes and then turned to idle away. One of the three 'fish' connected, blowing one of the enemy vessels out of the water. DuBose and his cohorts

were immediately taken under heavy fire for their efforts. Not surprisingly, Allan had been correct when he earlier elected to let these ships slip by so as to engage one group at a time – for it was indeed an escort group of the dangerous Flak-lighters. The three PTs immediately opened their throttles to retire and began laying smoke.

After regrouping, it was beginning to look as though the night's hunting was over when, after midnight, the radio station back at the Bastia base called Commander Allan with the news that an enemy contact stood between him and home, and could be located near the island of Capraia. Allan sent DuBose ahead with his scouting group to investigate. As nearly as could be determined by the three PTs, based on the scene painted by the sweep of their radar, the enemy force of three vessels seemed to be an ambush group intent upon putting an end to the Battle Group's forays to the mainland. There is some evidence to suggest that what turned out to be two destroyers and an S-Boat were instead engaged in unrelated minelaying. As the three PTs approached to within about 2,500 yards, a sharp-eyed German lookout spotted the incoming group, and guncrews immediately went into action firing starshells over the mysterious intruders. Someone aboard the 202 boat was prepared for just this instance and fired a captured five-star recognition flare which must have at least caused the destroyers to have second thoughts, for the PTs continued their brazen approach without being fired upon. As DuBose came to within 1,700 yards of the enemy ships he decided that he had pushed his luck far enough. As four Mark VIII torpedoes hit the water the Higgins boats turned to retire. Within moments one of the destroyers, TA-23, was hit and the three vessels opened up on the fleeing PT-Boats with everything they had, undoubtedly infuriated by the trick. The German destroyer was so badly damaged by the action that she was shortly abandoned and sunk by one of the other German vessels.

As the tiny force returned to Bastia there was no further contact with the enemy that evening. For all the damage caused by this model of Allied cooperation, it had suffered no casualties and, incredibly, no damage.

Towards the end of April, just as the first successful 'Operation Gun' missions were taking place, united PT-Boat forces in the Mediterranean were beefed up with the arrival of two new squadrons. Both Squadron 29 with its new 80 ft Elco boats and Squadron 22 with its complement of 78 ft Higgins boats had been equipped before shipment from the United States with the new Mark XIII torpedoes and their special roll-off launching racks. Originally designed as an aerial torpedo, the Mark XIII was considerably lighter than the World War One-vintage Mark VIII but ran faster, was infinitely more reliable, and had more hitting power. Elimination of the bulky steel tubes needed to launch the delicate Mark VIIIs went a long way towards lightening the boats with a resultant significant improvement in top speed. Torpedo armament aboard the boats has already been discussed, so suffice to say now that all hands on the United States boats in the Mediterranean were happy to be rid of the old Mark VIIIs.

The months of May and June 1944 were profitable for American PT-Boats in the Mediterranean. One of the more notable actions occurred on the night of 23–24 May. The plan involved another 'Operation Gun' task force with two scouting forces consisting of PT-Boats and a main body made up of PTs, MGBs and the LCG gunboats, all of which would once again head for the happy hunting grounds off Vada Rocks. As one of the scouting forces, consisting of PTs 202, 213 and 218, moved up the coast, they picked up two radar contacts heading south. They were interpreted as being corvettes, and Commander Allan – in charge of the main

body – gave Ed DuBose – aboard the 202 – the OK to attack with his three boats. Using radar bearings, the three boats dropped all their torpedoes into the water and turned away. Watching in great anticipation as they moved out the PT-Boaters were rewarded when the leading corvette erupted with two solid hits. The first group headed for a rendezvous with the second scouting group, consisting of PTs 302, 303 and 304 (all of the boats in this action were Higgins 78-footers) led by Lt Commander Richard Dressling aboard the 302. As the boats made contact, their radar operators watched the first corvette disappear from the screens. Dressling then asked and received permission from Allan to attempt an attack on the second vessel. As he moved his three boats into position he decided to launch torpedoes at an extended range based only on radar bearings, this because he knew the gunners of the enemy vessel would now be eagerly awaiting this second attack. At a range of over 2,600 yards the three boats each fired two torpedoes. In time they witnessed a yellow flash which silhouetted the corvette. Weeks later it was learned that although this second corvette had indeed been hit and badly damaged, she had made it home, but only to be stripped and abandoned. Possibly as a result of this action, the German Naval Command in Italy made an urgent plea to the Luftwaffe for bombing raids on the PT base at Bastia, adding that if the PT-Boats based there could not be destroyed or otherwise deterred from their nightly activities, the entire German sea supply system along the Italian west coast was in danger of collapse. The end of that system was perhaps closer than the Germans realized.

Two weeks later a three-boat patrol out of Bastia was involved in another notable action. Lt Bruce Van Buskirk in PT-558 led PTs 552 and 559 (80 ft Elco boats) to patrol areas La Spezia and Genoa. Soon they picked up two radar contacts which were assumed to be corvettes. With their radar screens they tracked the two vessels for close on half an hour, hoping to come within firing range before being spotted. The three boats each launched two torpedoes and then turned to idle away.

The crew of the leading corvette probably never knew what hit them: the ship virtually disintegrated before the eyes of the retiring PT sailors. Before the second vessel could take evasive action it, too, was struck. This second ship soon began firing wildly into the night, though not even in the direction of the creeping PTs, and radar operators aboard the boats soon noted the disappearance from their screens of the second vessel. In fact

postwar records confirmed that the three PTs had sunk the two corvettes TA 26 and TA 30.

This attack was noteworthy in that it represented one of the closest examples of perfect PT-Boat operational theory to be found. The boats had all of the advantages. The three new Elcos performed flawlessly, as did their torpedoes. The fact that they had radar and the enemy did not was, of course, instrumental in the success. But the action does demonstrate the advantages of a well planned, meticulous stalk, performed with great stealth, which proved to be of great advantage to the boat crews, who slipped away without being fired upon, and also prevented the enemy from taking evasive action, which would probably have come at the first sight of torpedo boats.

After this action it would be some time before American PTs in the Mediterranean would find suitable torpedo targets – for they had done their job well. The Bastia-based squadrons would soon be moving north – and eventually up to the south coast of France. But there, too, torpedo targets would be hard to come by. The early months of operation were, however, testimony enough to the value of these efficient little weapons platforms.

During the late summer of 1944 things were beginning to wind down for the Bastia-based PTs. Elements of both Squadron 15 (Higgins) and Squadron 29 (Elco) can be seen in this photograph. Of particular note is PT-562 in the foreground which is carrying old Mark VIII torpedoes in Mark XIII roll-off racks. This is interesting because it had been maintained ever since the beginning of the war that the Mark VIII could only be launched from a tube, to prevent its sensitive gyro from tumbling. Later, as Mark XIIIs became plentiful and the boats seen here found themselves with a surplus of the old Mark VIII's, permission was given to launch the old torpedoes into enemy-held harbors for general harassment. Several of the boats equipped with the Elco Thunderbolt are also visible in this picture.

Luckily someone had a camera! During the invasion of Southern France a fully loaded glider was accidentally released from its tow plane too far out to sea to make the shore. The pilot managed to ditch the glider without serious injury to his passengers, and the wooden aircraft obligingly stayed afloat until two Higgins boats arrived on the scene. Aboard PT-562 seaman first class Michael Kalausky watched as the accompanying boat rescued the waterlogged troops.

PT-552 was a late series Elco 80-footer placed in service during October 1943 with Squadron 29. The boat participated in several actions with United States forces in the Mediterranean, one of particular note taking place on the night of 14–15 June 1944. In company with PTs 558 and 559, the 552 tracked two enemy ships for a half hour and then fired torpedoes with radar bearings only. The two enemy ships, which turned out to be corvettes, were both sunk.

7

Barge Busting to Victory

There were words the officers frequently used to describe the campaign along the seemingly endless coastline of New Guinea; grueling, exhausting, miserable. But the Japanese were here, and in no other theatre was there a more vitally important job for the Boats to perform.

After the battle of the Coral Sea in early 1942 in which a Japanese amphibious operation aimed at Port Moresby had been turned away, the battle for the island of New Guinea turned into a land struggle. New Guinea is a giant island – second biggest in the world next to Greenland. By far the greatest portion of the island is dense virtually impenetrable mountainous jungle. While the Australians had for years administered the bottom side of the eastern portion of the island, the Japanese had made a rapid and unopposed advance during the first months of the war along the long northern shoreline which had been nominally administered by the Dutch. After the denial of Port Moresby by sea, the Japanese next launched a campaign from their newly formed garrison on the northern shore to head inland and try to take their objective by a land assault over the mighty Owen Stanley Mountains. Allied troops met the enemy and fought a bitter struggle in the jungle, the campaign going on for many months under the seemingly intolerable conditions found in the island's interior. Finally, paced by tough Australian jungle fighters, the Allied troops began to get the upper hand in the fighting and by the last month of 1942 they had pushed the Japanese all the way back over the mountains and down to the northern shore at the eastern end of the island.

The battle for New Guinea now became largely a question of troops battling each-other along the northern shoreline. The Japanese had a string of garrisons stretching almost 1,500 miles back up to the western end of the island and they appeared determined to defend every inch of their newly acquired territory to the last man. But the troops fighting at the front – wherever that might be along the shoreline at any point in time – would have to be supplied and reinforced and the only practical way to do it was via barge

and lighter traffic along the coastline and with transports from the Admiralties and from the mighty Japanese stronghold at Rabaul on nearby New Britain. Allied air superiority soon eliminated the use of larger ships transporting troops from Rabaul and the Japanese supply effort for their troops on New Guinea fell almost exclusively to barge traffic traveling down the coastline of the island from the west.

One of the easiest ways to defeat an enemy is to deny him what he needs to fight – interrupt his lines of supply. But operations along the New Guinea coast presented a separate nightmare. Interdiction of the coastal traffic called for warships, but warships of standard displacement simply could not operate close in off the New Guinea shoreline. The island waters were festooned with more navigational hazards than virtually any other area in the world, many of which were uncharted. Night operations (the Japanese could not run the barges safely during the day thanks to Allied fighter sweeps) with deep-draft vessels were unthinkable.

The answer to this problem was obvious, and by the first month of 1943 PT operations in New Guinea were underway. The mission of the PTs was simple: support the ground troops by busting barges.

By the time the first boats arrived the heaviest ground fighting was taking place along the coast between the villages of Buna and Tufi. At first the PT forces consisted of a mixed bag of 77 ft and 80 ft Elco boats officially listed as detached elements of Squadrons 1, 2 and 6 operating as a de facto squadron. Though only six boats were available during January, there were, nonetheless, nightly patrols run from a newly established advanced base at Tufi, only a few miles from the front lines.

A few words about Japanese barges are in order at this point. As the ground fighting

along the coast intensified, the Japanese began a crash program of barge construction. While almost anything that could be made to float was employed, the most common type encountered was known as the *daihatsu*. Generally from 40 to 60 feet long, they could be of steel or heavy wooden construction and were most often diesel powered. They were armored with protective steel plates and most were heavily armed with automatic light cannon and machine-guns. They were also arranged so that troops being carried could bring their small arms to bear during a fight.

The very shallow draft of these vessels made them impervious to torpedoes, formerly the main weapon of the PT-Boats, so they had to be dealt with by gunfire. But the barges were an even match for the first PT-Boats to arrive in New Guinea. They could soak up a tremendous amount of gunfire before going out of action while the PTs were far more vulnerable to a few well placed rounds of 20 mm fire. At first the main advantages possessed by the PT-Boats were speed, maneuverability and the element of surprise. During the early months of 1943 it was soon learned that the best way to deal with barges was to hit them as fast and as hard as possible – before they could return fire.

The ground troops wasted little time in their methodical advance up the northern shore of the island, and throughout the entire campaign – which lasted some twenty-three months, the PT forces, from ever advancing bases, were in almost constant nightly action. From its humble beginning the PT command in New Guinea would swell to a full fourteen squadrons supported by several major bases as well as eight tenders. As their numbers and strength grew, PT-Boats would not only attack the enemy along the New Guinea coast, but in New Britain and the Admiralties as well. While it would be beyond the scope of this work to attempt to chronicle the entire

Top

An excellent view of PT-66 seen tied up along the Morobe River during May 1943. As a member of Squadron 8, this boat was in on the action along the New Guinea shore right from the first. Squadron 8 was originally planned as an all-Elco squadron equipped with new 80-footers. But before leaving home, the squadron was instructed to trade four of its new boats for four 77-footers of the Melville training squadron – one of these boats being PT-66. The idea was to give the personnel at the training center an opportunity to familiarize themselves with the newer boats. PT-66 enjoyed a long career, being delivered to the Navy when the war was less than one month old and finally being reclassified as a small boat in February 1945. Note the varying shades of green camouflage applied in the field.

Bottom

A view of the jetty at the entrance to Tufi inlet, the first PT advance base in New Guinea. From the inlet PTs could idle up a narrow winding river covered by high cliffs and lush vegetation which offered protection against marauding Japanese aircraft. The little facility was put into operation during December 1943. During March the following year the tiny base suffered a major conflagration when a native threw a burning cigarette into the water near the jetty where two boats were refueling. PTs 67 and 119 blew up along with a small Australian cargo ship, 4,000 drums of gasoline and six depth charges. The gas-soaked ground burned for over a day. With Allied troops advancing rapidly north along the coast, Tufi, like Milne Bay at the eastern tip of New Guinea, soon became a backwater area as newer bases were established further up the line. It was used only as an unmanned refueling stop throughout the remainder of the campaign for boats on their way to the major overhaul depot at Milne Bay.

PT-149 was one of the first boats to initiate operations in the New Guinea theater during February 1943. As one of the boats of Squadron 8, it operated from the first bases on the island at Milne Bay and Tufi. The 149 is seen here running at speed in the glassy water off the New Guinea shore.

Bottom Left
PT-149 was fitted with an early type of radar, the scanner being protected by a canvas cover. Looking aft from the bow, the crew of the 49 is seen here as the boat heads back to Morobe after a night of patrolling during July 1943. This boat was involved in a rather unusual action during July when, in company with PT-142, it ran into a force of some thirty armed barges attempting to run between New Britain and Finschhafen, New Guinea. The night was so dark and rainy that neither group was aware of the other's presence until the barges actually began bumping into the PTs. The PTs immediately opened fire and sank six of the barges, but the 149 was itself hit in the engine room, a 20 mm shell cutting water lines, electrical connections and punching holes in the exhaust stacks.

Top Right
After the barge traffic in New Guinea dried up PT-149 ended up in the Philippines, but the boat, along with the rest of the squadron, saw no action after the New Guinea campaign. Like many of her sisters, PT-149 was stripped and destroyed at the end of hostilities, meeting a fiery end off the beach at Samar in the Philippines.

New Guinea campaign, out of hundreds of engagements a few of the typical as well as a few of the more noteworthy actions will be detailed.

One of the earliest actions fought by the PTs demonstrated right from the start that barges could be tough customers. On the night of 17–18 January 1943, an 80 ft Elco boat, PT-120, was patrolling off Buna when it encountered three Japanese barges. The PT roared in for the attack, 20 mm and .50 caliber guns blazing. But the Japanese returned in kind, 20 mm slugs ripping the PT and fatally wounding a sailor. After a brief but fierce engagement, two of the barges were finally set afire and the third disabled. It was obvious from the start, however, that more and heavier guns were needed to put the enemy out of commission as quickly as possible.

By March PT skippers were still trying to come up with the best method for dealing with barges. Lieutenants Skipper Dean of PT-114 and Francis McAdoo, Jr of PT-129 decided on the night of 15–16 March to try something they had learned back home while hunting in the woods. It was called the still hunt. They suspected that a tiny inlet along the Huon Gulf shoreline known as Mai-Ami Bay was used nightly as a barge terminal. The

PTs pulled into the area after dark and cut their engines to wait, hoping that the game would come right up to them. After waiting for some time McAdoo became impatient and decided to idle his boat back out into the gulf to see what he could find. The 114 waited it out, however, dropping her anchor to prevent the tide from washing her out toward the bay. Dean wanted to stay in close. What the PT sailors did not know was that a string of *daihatsus* had moved into the bay and were busily unloading all around the shore. As each barge was unloaded it would back off out into the bay and idle about in the dark. Although it may sound incredible that neither group knew of the other's presence at first, the situation becomes much more plausible with the addition of one other factor – rain. It was raining cats and dogs, and the beat of the squall on the water drowned out the noise of all the idling engines in the bay that night.

The first indication the men of PT-114 had that they might have been missing something is when two of the barges bumped harmlessly up against the hull of the PT. The men of the 114 froze. But the Japanese aboard the two barges continued to chatter amiably among themselves, apparently believing that what they had hit was simply another barge. The

Top Left
Natives help roll fuel drums aboard PT-133 while the boat is tied up at the Tufi jetty. Note the sailor in the background smoking.

Bottom Left
In one of the classic PT-Boat photos of World War Two, a group of the wooden wonders lie nested along the banks of the Morobe River in early 1943. The photograph was taken from the bow of PT-132, an Elco 80 ft boat named *Little Lulu*. Across the river is PT-68, one of Squadron 8's 77-footers formerly with the Melville training squadron. Ahead of PT-68 is the distinctly different shape of another Elco 80-footer.

Top Right
A Morobe-based Elco 80-footer idles out into the river with a group of locals embarked during early 1943. The first 80-footers to serve in New Guinea were in stock configuration with 21 in. torpedo tubes and the single 20 mm on the stern, as is seen on this boat. The first additions were extra .50 caliber machine-guns set up on the bow – to deal with barges. It was soon evident that more firepower was needed.

PT's gunners would have opened up immediately but the barges were so close that none of the fixed guns could be depressed enough to bear. Sub machine-guns were quietly passed around, and at a given signal the men opened fire. The PT started her engines, and one of the men cut the anchor line with an axe, allowing the boat to move slightly away from one of the barges which was then shredded by fire from the aft .50 caliber turret. The other barge, however, caught under the bow of the PT. Dean wasted no time in making his decision – he wanted out of this situation. He jammed the 114's throttles forward and rode up over the top of the barge, breaking it in two.

As the 114 swung around to make a firing run on the beach the 129 came roaring in alongside to see what all the fuss was about. The two boats then proceeded to dispatch the remaining four barges in the bay.

By July much of the action had moved further up the coast to Huon Gulf. Some of the boats by now had begun mounting the 37 mm cannon from P-39 fighters on their bows as a means of achieving increased firepower against the barges, the traffic in which was now really beginning to pick up. One of the more unusual actions fought during that month occurred on the night of 28–29 when two PTs, the 149 and 142, stumbled on a flotilla of over thirty loaded barges apparently making the trip across the narrow channel from New Britain to resupply troops on New Guinea. Once again it was dark and raining and neither force was aware of the other's existence until, with the two PTs apparently in the middle of the Japanese convoy, the PT sailors began to notice small signal lamps blinking all around them. In return to the apparent enquiries, the two PTs opened up with all guns. A blazing gun duel went on for several minutes, the barges returning heavy fire which damaged both of the boats. Several of the barges attempted to ram the PTs, one being sunk only ten feet from the 149. Realizing that in a fight with so many barges the boats were bound to suffer heavy damage sooner or later, the two skippers pulled away from the formation after having sunk six of the barges. Such was night combat in New Guinea.

The PTs needed still more firepower. During the month of August 1943 Squadron 12 arrived in the combat area with four of its boats equipped with 40 mm Bofors guns in place of the aft 20 mm. They had been so mounted before leaving the United States as an experiment. Another squadron, jealous of the installations, obtained additional Bofors

Top Left
Fuelling of a PT from an advance base in New Guinea could be a true exercise in ingenuity. Here some local natives lend a hand to the operation. Making the locals understand that cigarettes and gasoline were a fatal combination was a never-ending battle.

Bottom Left
With his boat tied up to the bank of an inlet on Morobe Island, New Guinea, during July 1943, a gunner strips his 20 mm Oerlikon gun to perform maintenance.

Top Right
A fine aerial stern view of PT-337 running off the New Guinea Coast. Close examination of the photograph will reveal that the base supports for the old torpedo tubes are still in place even though the boat has been field converted to carry Mark XIII torpedoes. During the night of 6–7 March 1944, while operating from the advance base at Saidor, PT-337 in company with the 338 cruised into Hansa Bay, a known enemy strongpoint, to raise some trouble. The answer was a direct large-caliber shell hit in the 337's gas tanks. The boat was lost along with several of the crew who apparently fell into the hands of the Japanese. Five crewmen were rescued after floating for a week in the PT's little balsa raft.

Bottom Right
A Higgins 78 ft PT at speed during a night patrol off New Guinea. Operational photography of PT-Boats is a rarity due to the fact that virtually all actions took place at night.

guns from the Australians and mounted them on their boats. Within a few months every boat in the combat area had its own 40 mm gun installed and the modification soon became standard from the factory. Some of the earlier boats removed their two after torpedo tubes to facilitate the installation of the gun, this bringing the weight back down to an acceptable level. Not a great deal was lost for the opportunity to fire a torpedo at the enemy for the enemy was rare in New Guinea. Although the introduction of the Mark XIII torpedo with its light-weight mount allowed four torpedoes to be carried along with the 40 mm gun, boats often went out on patrol with no torpedoes in their racks at all. Just as often, however, these boats carried extra crewmen and bristled with additional deck mounted machine-guns to bring every possible ounce of firepower the boats could carry into play against the barges.

The overall plan for the conquest of the Pacific by the Allies could not wait for the north shore of New Guinea to be swept clean of Japanese, so here, as elsewhere in the Pacific, leap-frogging was instigated. The only problem was that the Japanese troops which had been bypassed had to be contained and eventually starved out by virtue of their lines of supply being cut. This is exactly how many New Guinea PT-Boats managed to engage in some of the heaviest small craft gun duels on record, often in locations hundreds of miles behind the 'front lines'.

By September 1943 the campaign to rid the Huon Gulf area of Japanese was entering its final phase with the planned landing of troops at Finschhafen. PT-Boats were given the assignment of protecting the amphibious forces from any possible naval interference. So it was that Lt Commander John Harllee, commander of Squadron 12, was out on the night of 21–22 September riding in PT-191 along with PT-133 skippered by Lt Robert Read. About ten miles off Vincke Point the two boats encountered, of all things, a 120 ft Japanese cargo ship fully loaded and apparently making a run for New Guinea. Ensign Rumsey Ewing, skipper of the 191 reported:

'Upon sighting the ship, PT-191 followed by PT-133 closed in at high speed and then slowed to make a firing run to starboard. Light machine-gun fire was encountered on this run, but none thereafter. After the first run, two more runs were made at closer ranges and fire was directed inside the boat as much of previous fire had glanced offside. After the third run, the ship caught fire and lost headway, the PTs laying off in case of an explosion. Attempts to extinguish the blaze were observed on the ship. Another run and

depth charge set at 30 feet was dropped, but was a little too far off to be destructive. About seven men attempted to embark in a dinghy and this was sunk, the men either regaining the ship or jumping into the water. Although the ship was well ablaze and had settled, it did not appear to be going to sink and another depth charge was dropped close to the bow, blowing it out of the water and apparently breaking the keel. When last seen she was low in the water and still burning. It is considered that she was destroyed beyond further use.'

Within one hour of this action Allied troops were storming ashore at Finschhafen, the first phase of the retaking of the northern shore of New Guinea now almost complete with the expulsion of Japanese forces from the Huon Gulf area.

October saw an even more intensified barge production and use program by the Japanese, their High Command seemingly more determined than before that the Allied advance along the northern shore should stop. During this month from yet another advanced base at Morobe, the PTs claimed to have destroyed nine barges. The next month the total rose to forty-five. There were several factors involved in the dramatic increase. Certainly there was an increase in traffic, but more boats were beginning to arrive in the combat area, most of them now armed with the 40 mm Bofors. Moreover, the boats were employing new tactics which called for them to run along the coast much closer to the shoreline. The risks were obvious, and several boats were lost due to having their bottoms ripped out on rocks and reefs, but with the extra boats on hand it was felt that the risk was worthwhile, the PTs now missing far fewer of the barges than when they were running their patrols further out. One final and decisive factor was also coming into play – radar. Many of the boats were fitted with radar sets designed especially for use aboard PT-Boats and it made barge hunting ever more so productive. Naturally, the Japanese had no such luxury.

During December Allied troops went ashore along the southern coast of New Britain, and although this was far from the massive base at Rabaul the Japanese reacted violently. PT-Boats were soon sent to operate from the area of the landings, a small village called Arawe. An interesting action which took place soon after their arrival served to cast doubt on an established doctrine which said that if aircraft caught PT-Boats in the daylight it was all over for the boats.

While cruising some fifteen miles from their base, PT-191 commanded by Ensign Rumsey Ewing and PT-190 skippered by Lt Henry Swift were suddenly set upon by an

estimated forty Japanese fighters and dive bombers. The men aboard the boats figured they'd had it but weren't about to go down without a fight. As the Japanese broke off in groups of two and three aircraft to make strafing and bombing runs while the other waited their turns overhead, the PTs zigzagged wildly, often waiting until after a bomb had been released before breaking into a hard turn, the bomb always just missing on one side or the other. With each pass the PT gunners put up a tremendous volume of fire, blowing four of their attackers out of the air, one of them very possibly being the squadron leader for, as an executive officer later reported, 'Toward the end of the attack, the enemy became more and more inaccurate and less willing to close us . . . the planes milled about in considerable confusion as if lacking leadership.' Or it may have been that the pilots were simply not anxious to fly into the face of concentrated fire from the speeding boats. Whatever the reason, the boats made good their escape, thanks in no small part to the arrival after about forty minutes of battle, of a group of United States P-47s which quickly dealt with the remaining Japanese aircraft. Forty enemy planes had attacked two wooden torpedo boats and had failed to cause even serious damage to either, although the boats were peppered by shrapnel from near misses. Who said PTs could not survive in the open against aircraft?

By January 1944 the Allies had landed further up the coast at a place called Saidor. Once again, PTs began stretching their patrols further up the coast. Ensign Joseph W. Burke, one of the higher scoring barge 'aces' in New Guinea, described a typical action that took place on the night of 8–9 January. Burke's PT-320 was accompanied by PT-323 with Ensign James Foran in command. According to Burke:

'At 2225, four barges were sighted one mile north of Mindire, about one quarter mile offshore and headed south. All barges were about 70 to 80 feet in length and one was definitely seen to be carrying troops. As the PTs closed for a port run, the troop carrying barge opened fire with light machine-gun fire and a huge amount of rifle fire. On the first run three of the barges were sunk, one exploding when hit by the 323's 40 mm gun. The fourth barge made the beach but was destroyed by the PT-320 on its second run. There was an explosion of what appeared to be ammunition on this barge. All barges had been loaded. The barges took no evasive tactics other than to head for the beach and to fire upon the PT-320, which was the lead boat.

'At 00.30 three barges were sighted about three quarters of a mile off the beach at

Top
The torpedo dump at Mios Woendi, the small island in Geelvink Bay that became the largest PT operating base in the New Guinea theater. Here a 'cherry picker' loads a Mark XIII on to a cart for transport to a waiting boat.

Bottom
A crewman aboard an Elco 80-footer operating off New Guinea stands ready at his twin .50 caliber guns. His shells will streak through the night, every fifth round leaving a brilliant red glow recording the trail of its flight over the darkened seascape.

Maragum, four miles north of Enke Point. By the time the 320 and 323 closed to attacking distance, the barges were a quarter mile from the beach, proceeding very rapidly. They were close aboard when both PTs opened fire, and there was no doubt about all three barges having taken plenty of hits. One was definitely hit by 40 mm. When the PTs returned immediately after the first run, none of the three was observed floating. However, three other barges were seen lined up on the beach, ramps down and sterns seaward. These barges were empty while the others were loaded. While destroying the three barges on the beach, a shore gun that seemed to be about three-inch in size opened fire from a position two and a half miles north of Enke Point. Both boats proceeded to close in on the shore gun at high speed, firing .50 caliber, 20 and 40 mm shells. This caused the shore battery to cease firing at both PTs, and they proceeded to finish the task of destroying the beached barges. All barges involved in this action were 70 to 80 foot length.'

PT-Boats ranging up the coast of New Britain found much the same kind of action as the barge busters of New Guinea. During 1944, Lieutenant James Cunningham kept a diary, portions of which typify the kind of actions the nightly patrols would bring:

'March 12 1944: PTs 149 (*The Night Hawk*) and 194 patrol the north coast of New Britain. At 2300 we picked up a target on radar – closed in and saw a small Jap surface craft. We made a run on it and found out it was aground and apparently destroyed. We destroyed it some more.

'We moved to the other side of Garove Island, where we saw a craft underway heading across the mouth of the harbor. Over one part of the harbor were very high cliffs, an excellent spot for gun emplacements. We blindly chased the craft and closed in on it for a run. Just then the guns – six inchers – opened up from the cliffs on us, and it seemed for a while that they would blow us out of the water. We left the decoy and headed out to sea, laying a smoke screen. The concussion of the exploding shells was terrific. I still believe the craft was a decoy to pull us into the harbor, and we readily took the bait. The thing that saved us was that the Japs were too eager. They fired too soon before we were really far into the harbor. On the way home, about ten miles offshore from New Britain, we picked up three large radar pips and figured they were enemy destroyers, because they were in enemy waters and we were authorized to destroy anything in this grid sector. We chased within one mile, tracking

them with radar, and got set to make our run. We could see them by eye at that range and identified them as a destroyer and two large landing craft.

'We radioed for airplanes to help us with this valuable prize. Just as we started our torpedo run from about 500 yards away, the destroyer shot a recognition flare and identified themselves as friendly. It was a close call. We were within seconds of firing our fish. The task unit was off course and had wandered into a forbidden zone.'

By June 1944 the PT forces based at Aitape on the New Guinea coast were beginning to run missions during the daylight hours as well as their nightly patrols. This was made possible only because of Allied air superiority in the area, and indeed the PTs worked out a system whereby they were often escorted by fighters or light bombers. Based right at Aitape with the PTs were P-39 fighters and the rugged Beaufighters of the Australian Air Force and the two forces came to cooperate closely with one another.

One of the more successful of these daylight air escorted missions was made on the afternoon of 26 June. Lt Ian Malcolm in PT-130 and Ensign Paul Jones in PT-132 were patrolling when they received a radio message from escorting Beaufighters asking the

Top Left
When patrolling American PT-Boats surprised a group of Japanese barges unloading along a New Guinea beach in the black of night, this is the kind of scene air reconnaissance would find the next morning: wrecked barges and burned jungle.

Bottom Left
'Log dead ahead!' shouts the lookout on the bow of PT-331 as the boat speeds along the New Guinea coast on the way home from a patrol. An unseen log could cause severe damage to a prop or shaft, both items being in very high demand and short supply in New Guinea.

Right
Two sailors clean their boat's 40 mm gun while other crewmen rebuild their auxiliary engine. The auxiliaries were among the first items to break down, and spares were always in short supply. Connected to an electrical generator, the auxiliary engine powered such vital items as the electric stove and refrigerator as well as chartroom equipment and lights. When men lived aboard their boats, the auxiliary engine and generator were not simply luxuries – they were vital.

Elco PTs are seen here nestled up against their tender which has beached itself during the establishment of an advance base at Amsterdam Island during August 1944. Note the differing colors and patterns of the camouflage applied to boats of the same squadron.

Men shuttle equipment and supplies ashore during the establishment of an advance base on Amsterdam Island. The island is situated off the northern tip of New Guinea, in a perfect position for boats operating from the base to intercept barge traffic along the New Guinea coast during September and August 1944. Unfortunately the anchorage at the island was found to be less than suitable, and the site was eventually abandoned.

Because there was no shelter at Amsterdam Island, all of the necessary support equipment, such as the repair barge, floating dry dock and fuel tank barge, were simply run up on to the beach and anchored down as securely as possible. But storms and even stiff winds played havoc with such bases, and the men at Amsterdam fought constantly to keep the barges and boats from blowing up on the nearby reefs.

boats to investigate possible enemy activity on the coast of Muschu Island. The enemy was indeed there, but the boats had to close to within almost 200 feet of the shore before the crews made out two heavily camouflaged barges behind nets of fresh green foliage strung from the overhanging jungle which grew right down to the water. Realizing they were in the middle of a nest of barges, the boats immediately opened fire and made four passes up and down the beach. On their last pass, the crews counted some fourteen barges which had been riddled, six of which were ablaze. The fires spread ashore and apparently ignited an ammunition dump which went up with a tremendous explosion, and as the boats pulled away to return to base for more fuel and ammunition, flames from the fire could be seen with smoke billowing into the air.

When the boats returned bent on more destruction during the early daylight hours of the next morning, they were accompanied this time by four RAAF P-39s, each loaded with bombs for ground attack. The little combined forces intended to finish the job on Muschu Island. As the fighters droned overhead, the PTs made four more firing runs. They then backed off and fired their salvos of rockets (a weapon which was being increasingly installed on the boats in New Guinea) at a suspected supply dump with the anticipated devastating results. The rockets gave the PTs the punch of a destroyer broadside. As the boats withdrew, the P-39s went to work, making bombing and strafing runs and generally cleaning up.

Another favorite PT pastime was disrupting what little ground transport existed along the enemy held New Guinea coastline. Once again we turn to Lt Cunningham's diary, he having since been moved to the Aitape base:

'*23 June 1944*: PTs 144 (The Southern Cross) and 189 departed Aitape Base, New Guinea, for patrol to the west.

'We closed the beach at Sowam after noticing lots of lights moving. They appeared to be trucks, moving very slow. Muffled down, hidden by a black, moonless night, we sneaked to within 150 yards off the beach and waited for a truck to come around the bend and on to the short stretch of road that ran along the beach. Here came one, lights blazing. Both boats blasted away. The truck burst into flames and stopped, lights still burning. The last we saw of the truck (shore batteries fired on us immediately, so we got out) it was still standing there with headlights burning and flames leaping up in the New Guinea night. It has become quite a sport, by the way, shooting enemy trucks moving along the beach with lights on. The Japs

never seem to learn. We fire at them night after night. They turn off their lights briefly, then they turn them back on again when they think we have gone. But we haven't gone. We shoot them up some more, and they turn off the lights again. And so on all night long.'

But apparently the Japanese were not quite as unlearning as the young lieutenant thought, for his log of three nights later tells a different tale:

'*26 June 1944*: PTs 144 and 149 left Aitape Base, New Guinea, to patrol toward Sowam Village, where the road comes down to the beach. We were after trucks. We closed cautiously to three quarters of a mile off the beach, then it seemed that everything opened up on us, 50 and 30 calibers, 40 mms and three-inchers. At the time they fired on us we were dead in the water, with all three engines in neutral. To get the engines into gear, the drill is to signal the engine room where the motor mack of the watch puts the engines in gear by hand. There is no way to do it from the cockpit. Then, when the gears are engaged, the skipper can control the speed by three throttles.

'I was at the helm in the cockpit when the batteries opened fire, and I shoved all three throttles wide open, forgetting that the gears weren't engaged. Of course, the boat almost shook apart from the wildly racing engines, but we didn't move. The motor mack in the engine room below wrestled against me to push the throttles back. He was stronger than I was and finally got the engines slowed down enough to put them into gear. *Then* we got moving fast. We made it out to sea OK without being hit, but I sure pulled a boo boo that time.'

Continuing their leap-frogging strategy, Allied troops had moved further up the New Guinea shore by June 1944, and while Lt Cunningham was still shooting up trucks to the east, the PT forces were making themselves at home at their new base hundreds of miles to the west on the small island of Mios Woendi and were soon ready to begin operations in the great Geelvink Bay, primarily in support of the Army's effort to take nearby Biak island, also in the bay. It looked as though someone had designed the island of Mios Woendi with PT-Boats in mind. A deep water lagoon rose to flat sandy beaches and the base soon became the largest of all PT facilities in all of New Guinea.

Although the barge-busting activities were not as profitable as the earlier Aitape patrols, there was still plenty of action for the PTs during June and July. At first the Japanese attempted to resupply their troops on Biak with barge convoys from the north shore of Geelvink Bay, but the PTs harassed these

efforts to the extent that they were largely ineffectual. By the time the ground troops had routed the Japanese on Biak, the PTs were having to range to the northern shores of the bay to find targets.

The month of August 1944 was by far the most profitable for the barge busters of Mios Woendi, some twenty-six enemy craft being claimed as destroyed by the PT forces. It was also in early August that the last amphibious landings took place on New Guinea. The enemy were virtually routed from the Geelvink Bay area and were moving in headlong retreat to the northern tip of the great island. The Army staged landings near Cape Sansapor with the primary intention of securing an area large enough for the construction of an airfield from which missions could be staged against the next target in the island hopping campaign – the Halmaheras. To support the land forces it was decided to set up a PT advance base just off the landing site on a tiny piece of land called Amsterdam Island. On 2 August a small armada arrived at the tropical paradise, the force including LST 564, a floating fuel barge, floating repair barge, one floating drydock and PT Squadrons 24 and 25. The big LST, loaded with base supplies, rammed its nose into the beach, and men began pouring ashore to set up camp.

What the new PT forces of Amsterdam Island could not have known on that August morning was that life would be something of a trial during their two month stay at the base. As there was actually no natural bay or harbor on the tiny island, the base location was simply a likely looking piece of shoreline. But as the area was constantly buffeted by winds, there was the continual problem of boats and barges blowing on to offshore reefs.

Although the hunting wasn't anything like it had been in earlier months, the two squadrons accounted for eight barges and two 100 ft luggers during August. Traffic dropped off to virtually nothing in September although PT-342 did manage to find a rare use for its torpedoes on 22 September when it intercepted and sank a 200 ft minelayer, the largest enemy vessel sunk by the PT forces during the entire New Guinea campaign. At the end of September the base was abandoned, and the two squadrons returned to Mios Woendi. There were no targets of importance left in New Guinea by early November, and on the 16th of that month combat patrols were secured from the final operating base in the theatre – Mios Woendi also claiming the distinction of having been the largest PT base in New Guinea.

8

To the Philippines with a Vengeance

While other islands could be 'leap-frogged' and their Japanese garrisons cut off by American naval blockades, there was no question in anyone's mind that the Philippines would be taken. It was a matter of pride after the national embarrassment four years earlier. And in just as appropriate a manner, a powerful force of PT-Boats would return to the islands to bring havoc in the same waters where six small boats had stood so valiantly at the beginning of the war.

It was time for the Allied forces to go leap-frogging again. There was no doubt in anyone's mind that MacArthur had his eyes on the Philippines; he had made that clear enough. But from New Guinea to the Philippines was just a little too far – even for the redoubtable MacArthur – mainly because in between was the big island of Halmahera with some 40,000 Japanese defenders. Two things would have to happen before MacArthur could fulfill his promise of 'I shall return' to the Philippine Islands. First, the 40,000 Japanese on Halmahera would have to be neutralized. Second, the Allies were going to need an air base within striking distance of the Philippines to support the initial phases of the invasion.

Planners soon had the solution to the problem and it was simple: invade the small island of Morotai – only twelve miles across a narrow channel from the big island of Halmahera – and build a fighter and bomber base there from which to fly missions to the Philippines. At the same time the island would also serve as a naval base from which a sea blockade could be set up to make sure nothing either arrived on or left the island of Halmahera. It is not difficult to guess who was given the blockade assignment. On 16 September 1944, one day after the first landings on Morotai, the tenders *Oyster Bay* and *Mobjack*, with PT-Boats of Squadrons 10, 12, 18 and 33, pulled into their new home on the island to begin operations.

The PTs of Morotai would operate virtually until the end of the war from their base on the small island. With the original in-vasion of Morotai the existing Japanese garrison had been pushed back, and when the commanders felt they had enough breathing space to set up the naval and air facilities they simply stopped the advance, set up a perimeter and that was that. So until the end of the war there was still a Japanese garrison on the forty-mile-long island. Throughout the remainder of the war the command on Halmahera continually tried to reinforce their compatriots on Morotai – which could only be done by boat – and this made for continued good hunting for the veteran barge-busting PT crews.

Things were going so well for the Allied advance in the Pacific that Admiral Halsey recommended to Admiral Nimitz that the entire Philippine invasion operation be moved up two months ahead of schedule. His plan was to bypass Mindanao completely and invade the main island at Leyte Gulf. Nimitz checked with MacArthur and the plan was enthusiastically approved. The first landings in Leyte Gulf were to take place on 20 October and came off without a hitch under strong air cover and heavy naval bombardment from Admiral Oldendorf's line of old but powerful battleships which pounded the invasion beaches for hours before the landings. Once again, one day after the invasions, the PT forces arrived. Forty-five of the boats had been called up from Mios Woendi, New Guinea and had made the 1,200 mile trip on their own bottoms, being refueled en route as needed from escorting tenders. On 21 October, the night of their arrival, the boats were heading out to make the first PT-Boat patrols in Philippine waters since April 1942, when the last boats of the first Squadron 3 ceased operations.

For three nights the PTs ran patrols from Leyte Gulf, claiming to have sunk a small freighter and seven barges. But more action was coming. Steaming from the home waters of Japan were three powerful task forces, in fact the bulk of the existing Japanese combat navy, now committed and determined to put a stop to the Allied advance. They would engage an equally powerful force of American ships in what would come to be known as the Battle for Leyte Gulf, the biggest naval engagement of modern times.

The three Japanese task forces were converging on Leyte from the north, west and south, as was determined by air and submarine intelligence as of October 23. The force steaming from the north contained the enemy's carriers, targets that the aggressive Halsey could not resist. He took his powerful Third Fleet, with sixteen fast carriers and six of the new fast battleships to meet the northern force on 24 October. Unknown to him, this is exactly what the Japanese wanted. they were indeed wiling to sacrifice this northern force if it would allow the central and southern forces approaching Leyte, with seven battleships, thirteen heavy cruisers, three light cruisers and twenty-three destroyers, to pounce on the invasion fleet. The central force with five of the battleships and ten of the heavy cruisers was to enter Leyte through San Bernardino Strait while the southern force was to come through the Mindanao Sea and up through the narrow

PT-194 refuels at sea from its tender while en route from Palau to Leyte Gulf, where it would inititate operations in the Philippines.

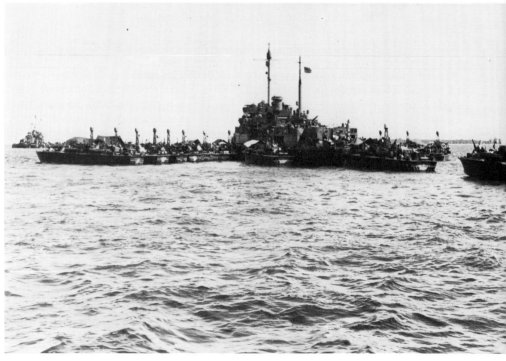

A view of a group of Elco 80-footers clustered around their tender shortly after arriving in Leyte Gulf and prior to the great Battle of Surigao Strait.

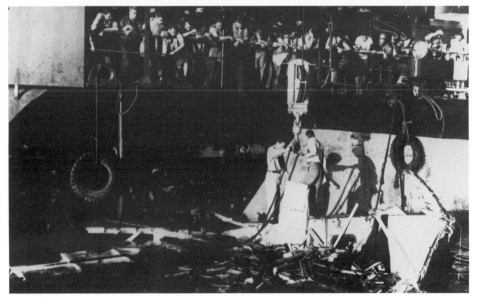

Top Left
PT-131, one of the earlier Elco 80 ft boats, is seen here preparing for the Battle of Surigao Strait in the Philippines, October 1944. She had only recently moved up from barge-busting duties in New Guinea as part of Squadron 7, and the profusion of deck-mounted weaponry needed for this type of activity is clearly visible. This boat was one of the first to make contact with the enemy in the coming massive sea battle. Among other weaponry note the field-installed barrage rockets which were good only for bombarding targets ashore. These were later replaced with a more sophisticated swing-out launcher.

Center Left
In the epic Battle of Surigao Strait in which 39 PT-Boats were deployed all along the enemy's approach route into Leyte Gulf, the very first boats to make contact with the Japanese included PTs 130, 131 and 152. As these boats attempted to move in on a group of Japanese ships which included a destroyer, two cruisers and two battleships, a light haze lifted, and Japanese lookouts spotted the approaching boats at a range of about three miles. This was much too far away for an effective torpedo attack, but the ships opened up with all guns. The three boats managed to turn and retire, but not before a 4.7 in shell burst over the bow of PT-152, blowing away the 37 mm gun and killing the gunner. The PT caught fire and was fixed in the searchlight of a pursuing destroyer which followed for over twenty minutes until depth charges and 40 mm gunfire from the PT forced the enemy ship to break off the chase.

Bottom Left
Early on the morning of 5 November 1944 a high-flying Japanese light bomber dropped a bomb over Leyte Gulf that landed squarely on the deck of PT-320. The boat was totally demolished, as this photograph attests, and two officers and twelve men were killed aboard the boat. It was an incredibly lucky shot on the part of one Japanese pilot.

Top and Bottom Right
Two views of PT-130, an Elco 80-footer bearing the name *New Guinea Krud*, as she cuts through Philippine waters on Christmas day 1944. This boat enjoyed a long and active career, serving throughout the New Guinea campaign on into the Philippines (including the Battle of Surigao Strait) and finally doing a tour patrolling the coast of Borneo as the war drew to a close. Note that one of the photographs was taken from atop the dayroom roof just ahead of the rear .50 caliber machine-gun turret of another Elco 80 ft boat.

passage known as Surigao Strait. Through a colossal oversight the central force was allowed to pass through San Bernardino Strait and enter Leyte Gulf unopposed. Between the American transports supporting the invasion and the devastatingly heavy Japanese force stood only a few escort carriers and destroyers. Someone had left the back door open. The United States command was under the impression that Halsey had left sufficient forces guarding the invasion beaches to handle any situation, but through misunderstood communications this was clearly not the case. Admiral Kurita with his central striking force had a tremendous victory in his grasp – as planned. As he came within range of the few remaining protective forces, aircraft from the escort carriers hit him with all they had, followed by a charge from the destroyers on hand. Kurita engaged and managed to gun down two of the escort carriers and three of the destroyers, and then, incredibly, he turned his mighty force around and headed for home, apparently happy to have destroyed the tiny escorting force. It was one of the most incalculable blunders of World War Two.

But what of the southern striking force? Admiral Jesse Oldendorf was given the responsibility for this group, and with his elements of the Seventh Fleet the battleship admiral laid out a plan designed to cut the Japanese to pieces. On the night of the 24th he dispersed his six old battleships across the northern mouth of the Surigao Strait to lie in wait for the Japanese with their two battleships and three heavy cruisers. It was the perfect setup. With no maneuvering, Oldendorf would automatically cross the enemy's 'T' in the classic battle-line sense. The Americans could bring all their guns to bear on the enemy column as it came up the strait single file while the enemy could only return fire from his forward batteries. But Oldendorf would take nothing for granted. He deployed destroyers in front of his battleships to make torpedo runs on the enemy and, even further down the strait, he ordered thirty-nine PT-Boats to line the shores and perform two functions. Disposed in groups of three – the farthest group actually stationed out beyond the entrance to Surigao Strait more than a hundred miles from Oldendorf's battleships – the PTs were to report successively the position and composition of the Japanese forces as they passed by; and then they were to attack.

Although the PTs were equipped with radar on the evening of 24 October, it was a clear night, and as each group of PTs moved in on the passing Japanese ships they were taken under heavy fire which beat them back

out of range. There was no essential element of surprise for the PTs as the Japanese crews were already alerted. By the time the action was over, thirty of the thirty-nine boats had been under enemy fire and ten were hit. Only one boat was lost, this being PT-493 which went up on a reef after being heavily hit by shellfire. Fifteen boats fired thirty-five torpedoes that night of which seven were claimed as hits. A few of the successful actions are described below.

*   *   *   *   *   *

Guarding the southern entrance to the strait were three PTs including the 137 skippered by Lt Isadore M. Kovar. The 137's auxiliary generator had failed before the action began, so it was without radio or radar. Around midnight the three boats saw flashes of gunfire in the distance, the Japanese were firing on PTs further up the line. The three boats separated and began tracking the approaching targets independently. Idling along, two screening destroyers almost slipped by Kovar in PT-137 before he spotted them and managed to fire one torpedo in an overtaking shot – a miss. The 137 idled about for another two and a half hours and then suddenly spotted another destroyer, this one coming back down the strait. Kovar maneuvered his boat to within 900 yards of his target without being spotted. At that point he fired one torpedo which ran hot and true and 'was observed to pass under the beam of the destroyer'. But nothing happened. There was no geyser, no flame. But, inexplicably, as the destroyer opened fire on the now discovered PT, all hands suddenly felt a heavy underwater explosion. Unknown to the men of the 137, their single torpedo had passed under the destroyer and continued to run until it hit another obstruction – the hull of the light cruiser *Abukuma*. The explosion killed thirty men and so damaged the ship that she had to fall out of column. The disabled ship was sunk two days later by air force bombers.

Stationed in the middle of Surigao Strait about ten miles north of Kovar's PT-137 were three boats led by Lt John McElfresh in PT-490. With him were PTs 491 and 493 skippered by Lts Harley Thronson and Richard Brown. As the Japanese battleships and cruisers approached their position, the three boats picked up the force on their radar sets about eight miles out. As the boats moved in they were engulfed in a rain squall which enabled them to approach to within 700 yards without being seen. At that point, several enemy ships were made out including one cruiser and three destroyers.

McElfresh in PT-490 launched two torpedoes at this range, aiming for the lead destroyer. At the same instant one of the other ships turned on its powerful searchlight, catching the PTs in its beam and opening fire. The 490 continued its approach to within 400 yards of the leading destroyer, fired two more torpedoes and opened up with all guns, shooting out the searchlight of the second ship only to be illuminated by another ship. One hundred yards behind the 490, PT-491 fired two torpedoes at the second destroyer. Both boats then turned away to retire under heavy enemy fire. As they ducked behind a smoke screen being laid by the 493, Brown later reported that he saw a flash and heard an explosion on one of the destroyers causing the searchlight to go out. Whether an enemy destroyer had in fact been struck by a torpedo has never been confirmed. As the boats pulled away, the 493 was hit twice by 4.7 in. shells, killing two of the crew. The boat finally made it to a reef off Panaon Island where she went aground and was abandoned the next morning. The 490 was also hit but remained on patrol until the next morning when the boat was attacked by four enemy dive bombers. Two of the planes dropped bombs which missed; the other two aircraft were driven off by the 490's intense anti-aircraft fire.

Furthest north of the boats deployed on the evening of 24 October were two sections: one led by Lt G.W. Hogan included PTs 320, 330 and 331 while the other, led by Lt H.G. Young, consisted of PTs 328, 323 and 329. These boats were stationed south and east of Amagusan Point on Leyte. As the American destroyer sections engaged in the battle sped down the strait making their torpedo attacks, these six boats were ordered to stand clear. The boats spent the rest of the night uneventfully, and in the darkness PT-323 under Lt Herbert Stadler became separated from the other boats in his group. Just after daybreak Stadler spotted a large burning Japanese battlewagon a few miles to the south of his position. He nosed the 323 in for an attack. Standing near the battleship was the apparently healthy destroyer *Asagumo* and Stadler picked this ship as his target. In fact, the Japanese DD had already been damaged and was dead in the water. The destroyer

As shown in these two photographs taken on 4 October 1944, when MacArthur finally returned to the Philippines he did so the way he left – aboard a motor torpedo boat. In the first picture the General's party disembarks from a cruiser to board the honored boat, PT-525, an Elco 80-footer. In the second photo the General stands on the bow as the boat heads for the Leyte beach.

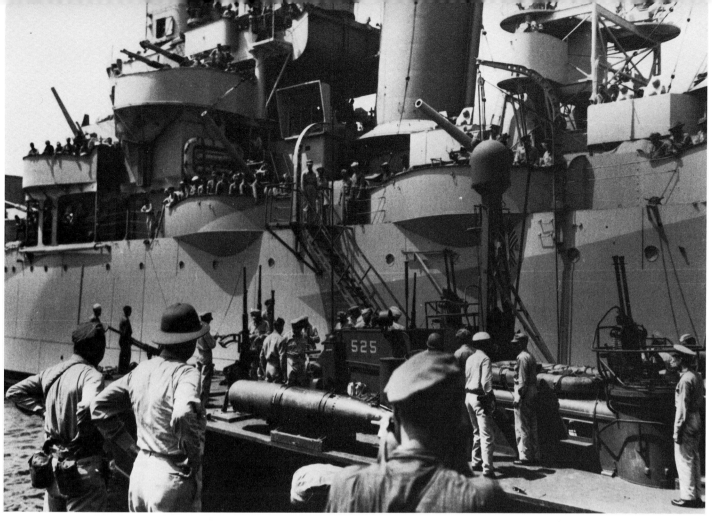

began firing at the speeding PT at 3,000 yards but Stadler pressed on. At 1,500 yards Stadler swung the 323 into a series of three torpedo runs, launching one torpedo on each pass. The third time worked like a charm, the crew of the PT being rewarded with a solid hit on the destroyer's stern. Even as the PT was launching its last torpedo, American destroyers were moving in to finish off the *Asagumo*, which sank forty-five minutes later.

The Battle of Leyte Gulf was the final blow for the Japanese Imperial Navy. The combined fleet could never again represent a threat to the overwhelming superiority of the Allied naval forces in the Pacific. But with the enemy now so close to the homeland, desperate measures were called for, materializing in the form of the *kamikaze*. These suicide aircraft singled out PT-Boats for targets on several occasions, tragically destroying two boats, each with heavy loss of life. PT-323 was dived on and hit on 10 December 1944, and PT-300 met the same fate seven days later. After the Battle of Surigao Strait, though no major naval action could be taken against the American invaders, Japanese ground forces on Leyte stiffened their resolve and fought fiercely against the advancing United States Army troops. The Japanese stronghold on Leyte was at Ormoc Bay, and it was from this point that supplies were distributed to the Japanese front lines. Ormoc Bay was, in turn, supplied from the other Philippine islands still in Japanese hands, reinforcements and material coming to a great extent from the big supply center on Cebu. This of course meant heavy waterborne traffic at night in the form of barges and lighters all the way up to full-sized transports. These resupply efforts were frequently escorted by gunboats, minelayers, destroyers and even an occasional cruiser. For the last time during World War Two the PT-Boats in the Pacific would enjoy good hunting. Patrols from Leyte Gulf naturally concentrated their attentions along the shoreline, often catching barges run up on the beach which would then be sunk with gunfire. But several actions involved torpedo firings as well.

One notable action occurred on the night of 9–10 November 1944 when Lt Murray Preston led PTs 492 and 497, one of several patrols being run that night, all the way around the island of Leyte to patrol above the Japanese stronghold at Ormoc Bay. At about 1.00 am three destroyers were spotted rounding the northern end of Ponson Island in the middle of the Bay. The two boats moved in and fired all torpedoes at the three ships in column. As the two boats continued south,

the last destroyer in column erupted with two solid hits followed by a bright blazing fire and dense smoke. The PTs were immediately taken in chase by the other two destroyers, lobbing shells and turning away only when the PTs ran dangerously close to the shoreline of Ponson Island. Before the attack Preston had positive radar identification on three destroyers, and as the boats pulled away only two remained. All hands witnessed the explosions on the ship; but once again, there was no confirmation for the victory.

After several more unsuccessful encounters with Japanese ships, PTs 127 and 331, under the command of Lt Roger H. Hallowell, sortied to Ormoc Bay on the night of 28–29 November. The boats encountered two Japanese ships of undeterminable type at the time. The 127 fired all four of its torpedoes at what was thought to be a warship. The 331 also launched two torpedoes at this target and then changed course slightly to launch its final two fish at the second ship. As the two boats dropped their torpedoes into the water they were taken under accurate fire by the two vessels. Retiring at full speed, men aboard both boats watched the two vessels suddenly erupt in violent explosions. Close behind the 127 and 331 came PTs 128 and 191. These two boats found three more ships at anchor in the bay. Firing seven torpedoes, the two boats witnessed a large explosion on one of the ships. It was later confirmed that in the first action PTs 127 and 331 had sunk a submarine chaser of some 200 feet in length as well as a smaller patrol craft.

The last big ship encounter of the Leyte operation came on the night of 11–12 December when PTs 490 and 492 executed a text-book attack on a single destroyer near Palomplon along Leyte's west coast. Picking up the target on radar at a range of about four miles, Lt Melvin Haines, leading the patrol in PT-492, inched the two boats down the coast, close in to shore so as to black themselves out against the jungle. At 1,000 yards Haines gave the order to fire, the 492 dropping two torpedoes into the water and the 490 firing a full spread of four. Seconds passed as the two boats awaited some reaction to their apparently undetected attack. Suddenly the destroyer blew up in two massive explosions, throwing debris several hundred feet into the air. The destroyer sank within seconds, three more heavy explosions coming after the ship had taken its plunge. It was later confirmed that the two boats had sunk the 330-foot *Uzuki*, a 1,315 ton destroyer.

Toward the end of December United States land forces were mopping up the last pockets of resistance on Leyte, this allowing

the PTs of Leyte Gulf to move to the other side of the island and adopt Ormoc as their new base. For the next three months Ormoc would provide a profitable jumping-off point for boats doing a lively business in barge busting, over 149 such craft going down under the guns of the boats from Squadrons 7, 12 and 25.

Mid-December saw the next phase of amphibious landings in the Philippines as United States troops stormed ashore on Mindoro accompanied by PT-Boats from Squadrons 13 and 16 which soon made themselves at home by setting up an advance base at Mangarin Bay. The Japanese turned their full attention to these landings, virtually all of their air-power being committed to retaking the island. The PTs participated in a number of engagements with Japanese aircraft and were responsible for downing some twenty aircraft in a matter of days. On 26 December the Japanese risked a small task force with the appointed duty of shelling the new United States airfield on Mindoro. American planes hit the enemy ships, a force consisting apparently of a battleship, a cruiser and six destroyers, thoroughly frustrating the bombardment mission. Several PTs attempted to intercept the Japanese ships but were taken under accurate fire and driven off. But one boat, PT-223, apparently unobserved due to heavy smoke, fired two torpedoes, one of which hit and sank the already damaged 2,100-ton destroyer *Kiyoshimo*, one of Japan's newest and biggest DDs.

Things were happening quickly in the Philippines, the United States forces soon consolidating their positions on Mindoro and moving in for the assault on the big island of Luzon during January 1945. Their strength drawing near to the twenty squadron mark in the Philippines, PT forces supported the operation by running patrols – often now during the day as well as the night thanks to American air superiority – up and down the Luzon coast destroying enemy barges as well as scores of the *Shinyo* suicide motorboats dispersed throughout hundreds of inlets all over the islands. The PTs did their task well. The *Shinyo* might have been a serious threat, but so many were destroyed in their hiding places that there is no record of any ship ever being damaged by one of the tiny craft.

As Allied forces retook Subic Bay toward the end of January, this marked the beginning of the final drive to liberate Manila. Appropriately enough, the first United States naval craft to enter Manila Bay since the PTs of the first Squadron 3 had been expended were PT-Boats of Squadron 21 and 27. And it was aboard a PT that General

MacArthur approached and landed on Corregidor on 2 March, 1945. The end of the campaign in the Philippines was close at hand, but one last task waited in store for the PTs in the area. With the landings of American and Australian troops on nearby Borneo, the PTs were called into action again to rake the shoreline with their gunfire, destroying hundreds more of the little suicide boats in their nests.

Lt Edward Pope, skipper of PT-134, watches approvingly as a crewman paints a railway car on the bridge of his boat – symbolizing a rather odd kill for such a craft. The action took place on the evening of 24 March 1945 when the 134, accompanied by PT-348, entered the heavily defended harbor of Cebu City on the island of Cebu, Philippines. The two boats approached to within 800 yards of a wharf where they spotted two freight cars and two barges tied up alongside. At that point machine-guns, a 37 mm cannon and a 75 mm cannon opened up on the boats. As the boats swung around, their machine-guns and 20 mm cannons opened up on the enemy gun emplacements while their 40 mm guns fired at the wharf. In moments the wharf was ablaze, and the boats made their escape.

The scene aboard an Elco 80-footer, PT-369, bearing the name *Sad Sack* during the Leyte Gulf operation. The gunner on the bow-mounted 37 mm stands ready to pump shells ashore should the boat pick up any fire from the beach. Note that with this later boat the plexiglass 'windshield' has been done away with in favor of a simple wind screen. Also note the large American 'stars and bars' painted on the top of the chartroom in the hope that aggressive but not exceptionally smart United States fighter pilots would be able to make the connection between the symbol painted on the fuselage and wings of their aircraft and the one painted on the boat below.

Top Left
PT-328 in the Philippines near the end of the war.
As part of Squadron 21 this boat saw action in
New Guinea beginning in October 1943. Painted in
Measure 31 camouflage (designed for inshore
operations), the boat is equipped with the latest
type of radar as well as swing-out rocket launchers
on either side of the bow. Use of the rocket
launchers usually meant that no torpedoes were
carried in the two forward racks. The large box
just ahead of the 40 mm gun contains ready
ammunition.

Bottom Left
The PT base at Babon Point on the island of
Samar in the Philippines grew to be the largest
PT base in the world as the war in the Pacific
drew to a close. It was near here that the majority
of the boats that served in the Pacific were
unceremoniously burned at the end of hostilities.

Top Right
This photograph was taken late in the war after
the invasion of the Philippines, and it is
interesting because of the weaponry on display.
Taken from beside the cockpit of an Elco 80-
footer, the subject of the photo is a 5 in rocket
which has just been launched from the starboard
wing rocket launcher. But also visible are two
20 mm cannons, a 37 mm cannon on the bow and
an 81 mm mortar. The mortar was found to be
particularly useful for lighting up an area with a
flare just before opening fire on an unsuspecting
barge that had been located with radar.

Bottom Right
An Elco boat silhouetted against the morning's
sun. Firepower and equipment borne by late 1943
virtually ruined the classic profile of the original
unencumbered 80-footer.

70 foot ELCO PT-BOAT

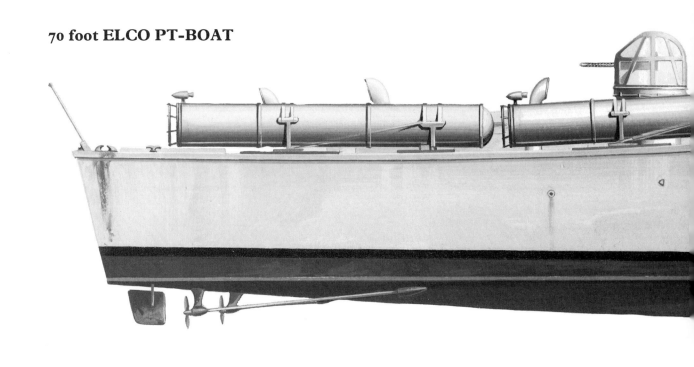

70 foot ELCO PT-BOAT (Top)

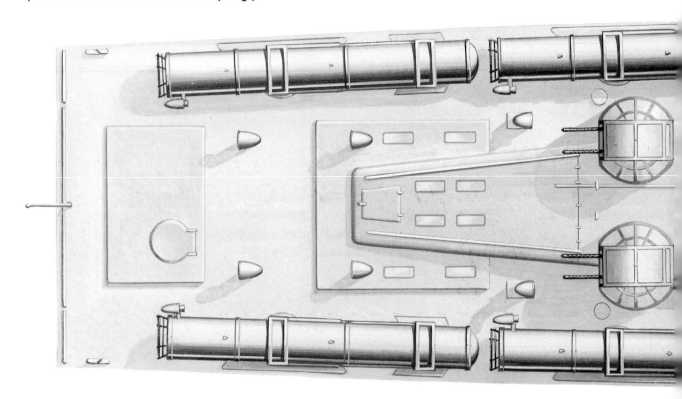

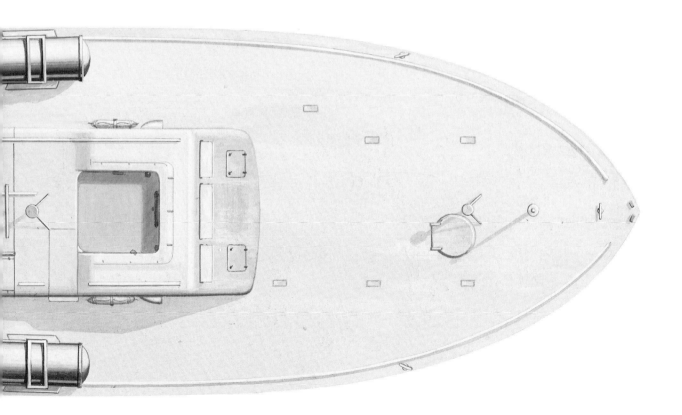

77 foot ELCO PT-BOAT

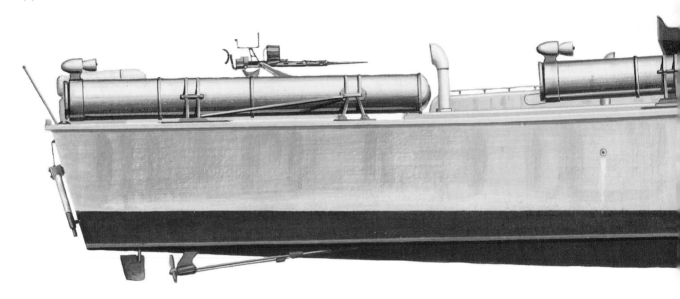

78 foot HIGGINS PT-BOAT

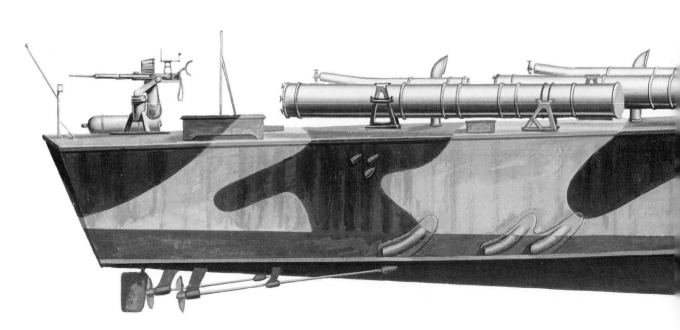

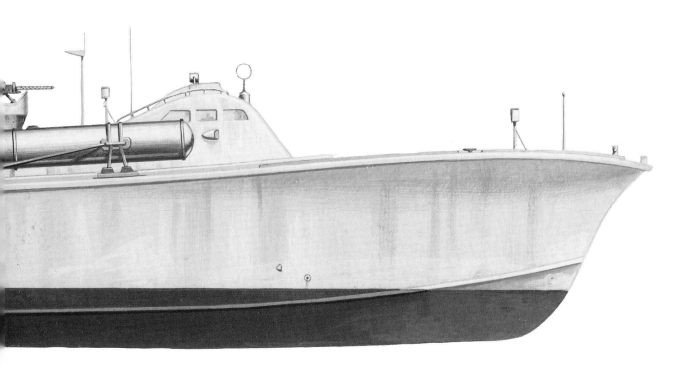

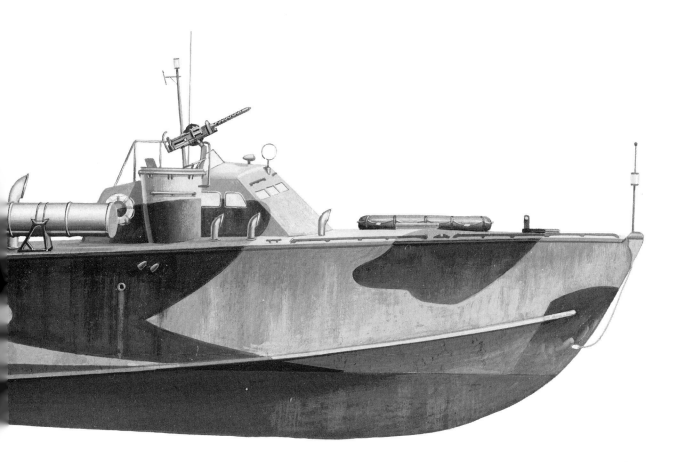

80 foot ELCO PT-BOAT

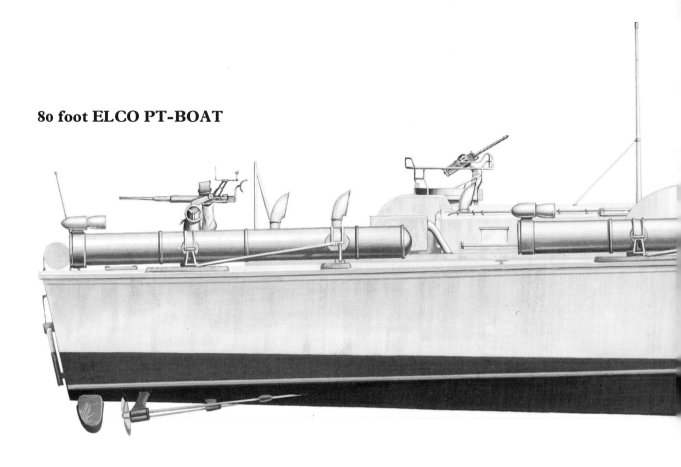

80 foot ELCO PT-BOAT

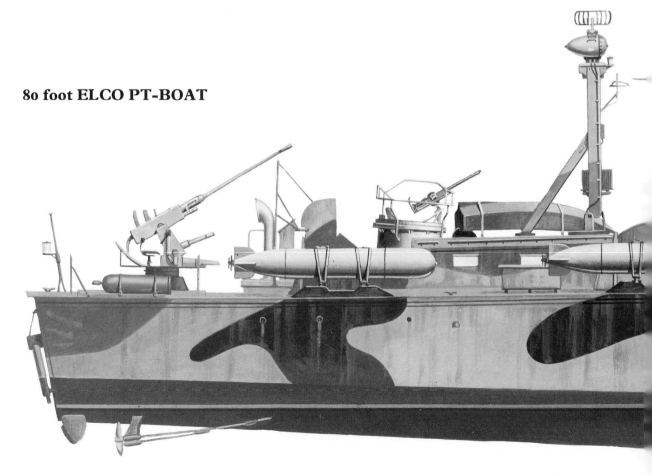

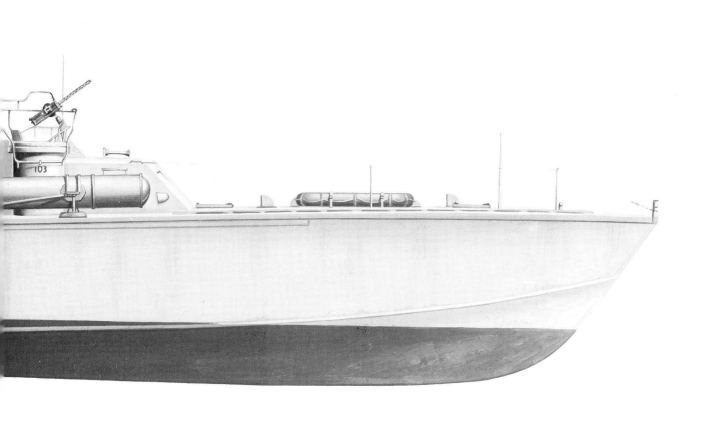

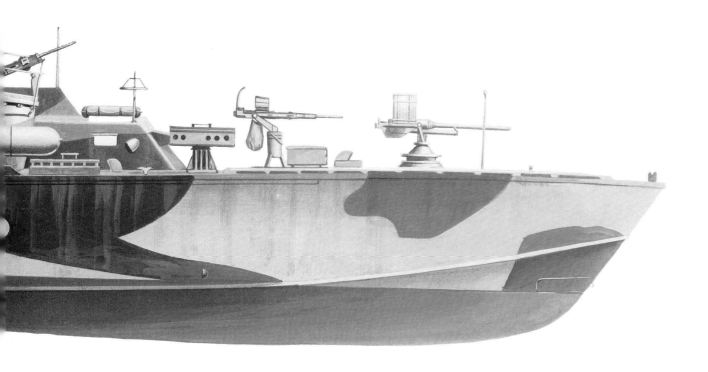

Epilogue

Even though the actions after October 1944 and on into 1945 were primarily those of patrol and destruction of barge and lighter traffic in the Philippines, the PT forces continued to grow, and by the summer of 1945 PT base 17 at Bobon Point, Samar, was the largest PT base yet built. Some 212 boats were operating in the Philippines and preparations were underway to use the boats extensively in the invasion of the Japanese home islands. However, such action was not necessary thanks to the dawning of the atomic age. By the end of 1945 all but three PT-Boat squadrons in service with the United States Navy had been decommissioned. Of the 212 boats on hand in the Philippines, 118 were inspected immediately after the cessation of hostilities and found to be defective. The boats were stripped of equipment and unceremoniously burned off a Samar beach. The remaining boats were disposed of by the Foreign Liquidation Commission, a few ending up in the hands of the South Koreans, who used them with some success against their brothers in the north a few years later. None of the boats in the Pacific were retained by the Navy.

The boats on hand in the United States, including those of the training squadron at Melville, were eventually sold by the War Shipping Administration, some of the boats going for as little as $5,000 each. By the end of 1946 only four new Elco boats remained on list with the navy and these were handed over to the South Koreans in 1952. These were the PTs 613, 616, 619 and 620.

As stated earlier the advent of radar on capital ships spelled the end of the torpedo carrying fast motor boat, radar controlled guns far outranging the effectiveness of a torpedo. Had PT-Boats been worth the effort? On that question there can be little doubt. There were absolutely no other forces in existence within the United States Navy capable of doing what the PTs did. In the beginning, they were on hand to interfere with the Japanese when American capital ship power was at a low ebb. In the Mediterranean, in conjunction with similar British forces, they interdicted enemy shipping that could not have been stopped by any other available means. Later, in the Pacific, they collared thousands of Japanese troops, rendering them useless to the enemy war effort by smashing their lines of supply. The Allies would have won World War Two without PT-Boats, but substantial numbers of additional lives would have been lost in the process.

Appendix

PT-BOAT BUILDING PROGRAM

1 and 2	Fogal Boat Yard, Inc.
3 and 4	Fisher Boat Works
5 and 6	Higgins
7 and 8	Philadelphia Navy Yard
9	British Power Boat Co. (Purchased by Elco)
10 to 68	Elco (10 to 19 70′ boat) 77′
69	Huckins experimental boat
70	Higgins (Dream Boat)
71 to 94	Higgins
95 to 102	Huckins
103 to 196	Elco 80′
197 to 254	Huckins
265 to 313	Higgins
314 to 361	Elco
362 to 367	Harbor (Elco model built at West Coast)
368 to 371	Canadian Power Boat Company
372 to 383	Elco
384 to 399	Jacobs (Vosper boats for Lend-Lease)
400 to 429	Annapolis (Vosper boats for Lend-Lease)
430 to 449	Herreschoff (Vosper boats for Lend-Lease)
450 to 485	Higgins
486 to 563	Elco
564	Higgins (Experimental Hellcat 70′ boat)
565 to 622	Elco
623 to 624	Elco (Contract cancelled)
625 to 660	Higgins (Lend-Lease to USSR)
661 to 730	Annapolis (Vosper boats for Lend-Lease)
731 to 760	Elco (Shipped to USSR)
761 to 790	Elco (Contract Cancelled)
791 to 796	Higgins
797 to 808	Higgins (USN contract cancelled but boats completed by builder and sold to Argentine Navy)

NICKNAMES OF PT BOATS

PT 4	Get In Step
PT 17	Monkey's Uncle
PT 21	Black Jack
	Sad Sack
PT 22	Flying Deuces
PT 24	Blue Bitch
PT 34	P.I. Rose
	Duece
	Eager Beaver
PT 45	Duce Boat
	Coughing Coffin
PT 59	Gun Boat
PT 65	Hogan's Goat
PT 77	Galloping Ghost
PT 80	Katydid
PT 82	Cutty Sark
PT 83	Reluctant Dragon
PT 84	Peacock Lounge
PT 88	Ivory Coaster
PT 99	Porkers Stern
PT 100	Sea Cat
	Sea Wolf
PT 102	Lazy Lum
PT 105	Hell Cat
PT 106	Devil Hawk
PT 107	Black Magic
PT 108	Plywood Bastard
	Lil' Duck
PT 109	JFK
PT 110	Hirohito's Headache
PT 113	Zero Chaser
PT 113	Green Banana
PT 114	Buccaneer
PT 115	Hogan's Goat
PT 117	Munda Morn
PT 118	Little Robbie
PT 120	Roarin' 20
PT 122	'Super Boat'
PT 124	Who-Me
PT 126	Miss Gwin
PT 128	Tug Boat Annie
	Hindri
PT 129	Gypsy Wildcat
	Artful Dodger
PT 130	Raven
PT 131	Tarfu
	Itarie
PT 132	Little Lulu
PT 133	New Guinea Ferry
PT 134	Lucky Alf
PT 135	'SNAFU'
PT 136	New Guinea Krud
PT 138	Green Bitch
	Thunderbolt
	Java Jive
PT 139	Zebra
PT 140	Hells Cargo
PT 142	Flying Shamrock
PT 143	Ring Dang Do
PT 144	Southern Cross

PT 145	Shark	
PT 146	Green Hornet	
PT 146	Lucky Lady	
PT 147	Stinky	
PT 148	Fertile Myrtle	
PT 149	Nite Hawk	
PT 150	Lady Lucifer	
	Princess	
PT 151	Wuncanitsenuf	
PT 152	Lack-a-Nookie	
	Miss Malaria	
PT 153	Leaping Lena	
PT 154	Mr. 'B'	
PT 155	5 × 5	
	Rapid Robert	
PT 156	Cowboy	
PT 157	Aces & Eights	
	Old Pickle Puss	
PT 158	Rendova Racer	
PT 159	Red Dragon	
	Red Devil	
	Janie	
PT 160	Lazy Daisy Mae	
	Tokyo Ahead	
PT 161	Jahnz Canoe	
	Sassy Sally	
PT 162	Wicked Witch	
PT 164	Fubar	
PT 167	Who Me?	
	Knickerbocker	
PT 168	Radin' Maiden	
PT 170	Zebra	
PT 171	Devil Due	
PT 172	Shamrock	
PT 174	Hickory	
PT 175	Miss Lace	
PT 178	Torpedo Junction	
PT 180	Marie	
PT 181	Rumdum	
PT 187	8 Ball	
PT 188	Carolina Queen	
	Cookie	
PT 189	8 Ball	
	Night Mare	
PT 190	Jack O'Diamonds	
PT 191	Bambi	
PT 192	Galloping Guillotine	
	'Martini'	
PT 193	Bitchin' Witch	
PT 194	Little Mike	
	Liberty Hound	
PT 195	Black Agnes	
PT 196	Purple Shaft	
PT 198	High on Windy Hill	
PT 201	Ace of Spades	
PT 202	J Square	
PT 203	Sharks Head	
PT 204	Aggie Maru	
PT 205	Rambling Wreck	
PT 206	Lonely Hearts	
PT 207	Big Seven	

	Lucky Seven	
	Zebra	
PT 208	Eight Ball	
PT 209	Pistol Packin' Mama	
PT 210	Little Poison	
	Marie	
PT 211	Night Owl	
PT 212	Cruisin' Susan	
	Sea Horse	
	Swiftly	
	Sea Mustang	
PT 213	Spittin' Kitten	
	Gallopin' Ghost	
PT 214	Little Killer	
	Zombie	
	Gallopin' Ghost	
PT 215	Man of War	
PT 216	Shangri La	
PT 217	Tresch Can	
	Red Falcon	
PT 220	Chow Down	
PT 221	Omen of the Seas	
PT 222	Three Deuces	
PT 224	Tail End	
PT 226	Hell Razor	
PT 227	Pink Lady	
PT 230	Sea Cobra	
	Mol Flanders	
PT 231	Red Devil	
PT 232	Holiday Routine	
PT 233	Green Sin	
PT 234	End Gate	
PT 235	Rebel	
PT 236	Crayfish	
	Crawfish	
PT 237	Battling Betty	
PT 237	Pistol Packin' Mama	
PT 238	Spinnin' Jennie	
PT 239	Dry Dock Annie	
PT 240	Jinx	
PT 241	Snuffy	
PT 242	Celeste	
	Crusin' Susan	
PT 243	Tonde Leyo	
PT 244	Werewolf	
PT 248	Vibratory	
PT 249	Scuflin Ass	
PT 251	Nola Flash	
PT 253	Panama Hattie	
PT 254	Cuba Lebra	
PT 255	Nix	
PT 256	Barfly	
PT 257	Idiots Delight	
	LaPutita	
	Miss Carriage	
PT 258	LaPutita	
PT 259	Little Joe	
PT 260	IGMFU	
PT 261	Lucifer Jr	
PT 263	SNAFU	
PT 264	Hogan's Goat	

PT 277	Knightmare	
PT 278	Bottoms Up	
PT 280	Scutter	
PT 282	Mail Boat	
PT 283	Hero's Haunt	
PT 284	Gunboat Annie	
PT 285	Scuttlebutt John	
PT 285	Fighting Irish	
PT 286	Rough Knight	
	P.I.P.	
PT 297	Old '97'	
PT 298	Big Time Charlie	
PT 299	Pom Pom	
	Two Ninety Niner	
PT 300	Kamakaze Val.	
PT 302	Dock Trotter	
PT 303	Hogan's Goat	
PT 304	USS Cherry	
	Seawolf	
PT 305	USS Sudden Jerk	
PT 306	The Fascinatin' Bitch	
PT 307	Sad Sac	
PT 308	La Dee Da	
PT 309	Oh Frankie	
PT 310	Alcyone	
PT 311	Wanderer	
PT 312	The Stray Lamb	
	Bacchante	
PT 313	Sea Wolf	
PT 316	Melville Express	
PT 318	One Way	
	Ole Pickle Puss	
	Sea Bisket	
PT 320	Sea Bitch	
PT 321	Black Jack	
	Hot Run	
	Green Horelet	
	Death's Hand	
PT 323	SNAFU	
PT 323	Jinx	
PT 325	Outlaw	
	Ala Baba and his 14 Thieves	
	Hot Run	
PT 326	Green Harlot	
	Carolina Chile	
PT 327	Hell's Half Acre	
	Mr Completely	
PT 328	Bayonne Bitch	
PT 329	Belle	
	Hell's Bells	
PT 330	Balzanol	
	Eager Beaver	
PT 331	Ramblin Wrecker	
	Wolf	
PT 332	Ferrett	
	Black Hawk	
PT 333	Hi-De-Ho	
	Green Beast	
	Thunderhawk	
PT 334	Barracuda	
	Victoria	

PT 335	Sea Hawk	PT 497	Many Pesos	PT 592	Old Black Crow
	Battle Bird	PT 498	Warmaster	PT 594	States Happy
PT 336	Relay Champ	PT 499	Miss Kate	PT 595	Hot Shot
PT 337	PT Intrepid	PT 500	Stratus	PT 599	Katcha Maru
	Heaven Can Wait	PT 502	Idiots Delight	PT 604	Tiger Shark
PT 338	Devil Chaser		Nasty Bastard	PT 605	Bounty
PT 339	The Vonie Marie	PT 503	What's Next	PT 606	Roxie
PT 340	Condegausser	PT 504	The Nasty Bastard	PT 613	Abracadabra
	Life Beginz at 40	PT 505	Diana	PT 617	Big Red Cock
PT 342	Death Hawk	PT 507	Hemmingway Hotel	PT 619	Soko Devil
PT 342	The Joseph Lynch	PT 508	Mairsey-Doats	PT 796	Tailender
	Tomahawk	PT 509	Sassy Sue		
	Logans Demon	PT 510	Bonnie		
PT 343	Pauline Too!	PT 511	Come Seven		
	Ahdocon	PT 513	Umbriago		
PT 345	Gallinipper	PT 514	Hoy Hoy		
PT 346	Bett B	PT 515	Boomerang		
PT 347	Zombie	PT 516	Flying Gini		
PT 348	Mary Mae	PT 517	Pug Mahon		
PT 349	Guinea Gal	PT 518	'Requisition Joe'		
	Bee Bee	PT 520	Coral Princess		
PT 350	Shifty Fifty		Coral Queen		
PT 352	Sarah	PT 521	Snapperette		
	'Sara'	PT 522	Paddy's Pig		
	My Littie	PT 524	Bet Me		
PT 354	Cruncher	PT 526	Return Ticket		
	Lip & Tuck	PT 527	Stork Club		
PT 355	Hells Cargo	PT 530	El Snatcho		
PT 356	Dianamite 6	PT 534	Sidewinder		
PT 357	Dianamite II	PT 537	Little Tomato		
PT 362	Geisha Gooser	PT 540	40 Thieves		
PT 363	Aces Avenger	PT 542	Margie		
PT 366	Hogan's Goat		Skid's Boat		
PT 369	J Mar J	PT 547	Paoli Local		
	Sad Sack		Ena Baby		
PT 372	Donna Faye	PT 548	Devil's Dozen		
	Miss Fortune	PT 550	Queen Bee		
PT 373	Hatches	PT 552	Hairless Joe		
PT 374	Torpedo Truk	PT 553	Marrin' Sam		
PT 375	Judy	PT 554	Moonbeam		
PT 376	Spirit of '76	PT 556	Daisey Mae		
PT 379	Scorpion	PT 559	Black Ruff		
PT 380	Hellion	PT 560	Lonesome Pole Cat		
PT 381	Shelly	PT 563	Mammy Yokum		
	George Matt	PT 567	Sea Jeep		
PT 390	Little Butch	PT 575	Prep Holiday		
PT 456	Hogan's Goat	PT 576	Yura Kaze		
PT 458	Stretch III		Night Wind		
	Hogan's Goat		Bitchin' Witch		
PT 459	Mahogany Menace	PT 577	Dianamite II		
PT 460	Ali Baba	PT 578	Bolo		
PT 461	Summa	PT 579	Gizmo		
PT 474	Cocky Four	PT 580	8 Ball		
PT 478	Hubba-Hubba		Lazy Eight		
PT 484	Snuffy Smith	PT 582	'HuChee'		
PT 485	The Saint		'Heller'		
PT 491	Ferdinand the Bull	PT 583	One Way		
	Devil's Daughter	PT 584	Gracie		
PT 492	Impatient Virgin	PT 585	Tojo		
PT 494	Blind Date	PT 586	'Thom Cat'		
PT 495	Gentleman Jim	PT 588	Dianamite III		
PT 496	Miss Fury	PT 591	The Pest		

Note: Nicknames of boats sometimes were changed as the crew was rotated. Some boats had no nickname.

Note: When a PT-Boat changed skippers the nickname was often changed as well, hence a number of the boats are shown as having more than one name.

LISTING OF MOTOR TORPEDO BOAT SQUADRONS DURING WORLD WAR II

Squadron	Campaigns	Type Boat	PT Boat Numbers
Ron 1	Pearl Harbor, Midway, Aleutians	77′ Elco	20–31, 33, 35, 37, 39, 41–43
Ron 2	South Pacific English Channel	77′ Elco 78′ Higgins	20–26, 28, 30, 32, 34, 36–40, 42–48, 59–61 71, 72, 199
Ron 3	Philippines South Pacific	77′ Elco 77′ Elco	31–35, 41 21, 23, 25, 26, 36–40, 45–48, 49–61
Ron 4	Training Squadron	77′ Elco 78′ Huckins 70′ Higgins 78′ Higgins 80′ Elco	59–68 95–102 564 71, 72, 199, 200, 295, 296, 450–452 139–141, 314–317, 486, 487, 505, 545, 557–559, 613, 616, 619, 620
Ron 5	Panama, S. Pacific Southwest Pacific	77′ Elco 80′ Elco	52–65 103–114, 314–319
Ron 6	South Pacific Southwest Pacific	80′ Elco	115–126, 187, 188
Ron 7	Southwest Pacific	80′ Elco	127–138
Ron 8	Southwest Pacific	77′ Elco 80′ Elco	66–68 110, 113, 114, 120–122, 129, 130, 142–150, 188, 189
Ron 9	South Pacific Southwest Pacific	80′ Elco	126, 151–162, 187, 318, 319
Ron 10	South Pacific	80′ Elco	108, 116, 124, 125, 163–174
Ron 11	South Pacific Southwest Pacific	80′ Elco	175–186
Ron 12	Southwest Pacific	80′ Elco	127, 145, 46, 150–152, 187–196
Ron 13	Aleutians, Southwest Pacific	78′ Higgins	73–84
Ron 14	Panama Sea Frontier	78′ Huckins	98–102
Ron 15	Mediterranean	78′ Higgins	201–218
Ron 16	Aleutians, Southwest Pacific	78′ Higgins	71, 72, 213–224, 235, 241, 242, 295–301
Ron 17	Hawaii Southwest Pacific	78′ Higgins	71, 72, 225–234
Ron 18	Southwest Pacific	80′ Elco 70′ Scott-Paine	103–105, 147, 148, 362–367 368–371
Ron 19	South Pacific	78′ Higgins	235–244

Squadron	Campaigns	Type Boat	PT Boat Numbers
Ron 20	South Pacific Southwest Pacific	78′ Higgins	235–238, 245–254
Ron 21	Southwest Pacific	80′ Elco	128, 131, 132, 320–321
Ron 22	Mediterranean	78′ Higgins	302–313
Ron 23	South Pacific Southwest Pacific	78′ Higgins	241–244, 277–288
Ron 24	Southwest Pacific	80′ Elco	106, 332, 343
Ron 25	Southwest Pacific	80′ Elco	115, 134, 344–355
Ron 26	Hawaii	78′ Huckins	255–264
Ron 27	South Pacific Southwest Pacific	80′ Elco	356–361, 372–377
Ron 28	South Pacific Southwest Pacific	80′ Elco	378–383, 546–551
Ron 29	Mediterranean	80′ Elco	552–563
Ron 30	English Channel	78′ Higgins	450–461
Ron 31	Pacific Fleet	78′ Higgins	453–455, 462–473
Ron 32	Pacific Fleet	78′ Higgins	474–485
Ron 33	Southwest Pacific	80′ Elco	137, 138, 488–497
Ron 34	English Channel	80′ Elco	498–509
Ron 35	English Channel	80′ Elco	510–521
Ron 36	Southwest Pacific	80′ Elco	522–532
Ron 37	Pacific Fleet	80′ Elco	533–544
Ron 38	Southwest Pacific	80′ Elco	565–576
Ron 39	Pacific Fleet	80′ Elco	575–588
Ron 40	Pacific Fleet	80′ Elco	589–600
Ron 41	Not shipped to Pacific	80′ Elco	601–612
Ron 42	Not shipped to Pacific	80′ Elco	613–622
Ron 43	Transferred to USSR	78′ Higgins	625–633
Ron 44	Transferred to USSR	78′ Higgins	637–648
Ron 45	Transferred to USSR	78′ Higgins	649–660

Index

Photograph acknowledgements:– John Batchelor: 24 Top, Center left; 28 Top, Bottom; 43; 50 Top; 55 Top, Bottom; 56 Top, Center, Bottom; 57 Top, Bottom; 58 Top left, Top right, Bottom; 59 Top right; 81 Top; 123 Bottom. – **Victor Chun:** 119 Top. – **E. A. DuBose:** 44 Bottom; 76 Bottom. – **Imperial War Museum:** 12 Top, Bottom; 13 Bottom; 18; 53 Top, Bottom. – **Michael Kalausky:** 121 Top; 123 Top; 146 Top. – **Public Archives of Canada:** 35. – **John Reilly:** 102 Top, Bottom. – **Captain Hugh M. Robinson:** 39; 41 Bottom; 83 Bottom; 98 Top; 100. – **Stanley Rosenfeld:** 14; 15. – **Robert L. Searles:** 26; 27; 84; 85; 88; 89; 93 Top, Bottom; 94; 96 Bottom; 97 Top; 99; 131 Bottom. – **U.S. Bureau of Aeronautics:** 78 Top; 130 Top, Bottom; 133 Bottom; 136 Top. – **U.S. Navy:** 2/3; 11; 17; 21; 22 Top, Bottom; 25; 28 Center; 29 Top, Bottom; 30 Top; 31 Top; 33 Bottom; 38 Top; 41 Bottom; 49; 50 Bottom; 54; 60 right, Bottom left; 61 Top, Bottom; 62 Top, Bottom; 63; 64 Top left, Top right, Bottom; 65 Center left; 74 Top; 77 Top; 113 Bottom; 117 Center; 119 Bottom; 120 Bottom; 125 Bottom; 128 Top; 133 Top; 135 Bottom; 139 Top, Bottom; 140 Bottom; 141 Bottom; 143 Bottom; 146 Bottom.